D0873517

MICHAEL PEDRETTI

Time

to

Journey

Home

Book I of a 12 part series titled

The Story of Our Stories

To my friend Anne
Michael Pedretti
10/23/2022

Pedretti, Michael 1942

–story of our stories: /pedretti

This book is sold subject to the condition that it shall not, by way of trade or otherwise be lent, hired out, re-sold, or otherwise circulated without the publisher's prior consent in any form of binding or cover other than that in which it is published and without a similar condition including this condition being imposed on the subsequent purchaser.

Busting Boundaries, Williamsburg, VA

"ISBN 978-1-54399-850-4".

I would like to first and foremost thank the mothers who time and time again planted seeds instead of discord; steering the sons away from war, violence and thievery. *Time to Journey Home* is dedicated to my ancestors whose lives inspired these stories. Special thanks to all who participated in research on the history of our family – especially to Jim Venner, Jean Pedretti-Flottmeyer, Anne Guerrieri, Luigi Fanetti, Dino Buzzetti and Alberto Cerletti.

I thank Dennis Hamilton who provided valuable feedback and multiple corrections on early drafts of this work. I would like to especially thank my wife, Nancy B. Hill, and daughter, Victoria Pedretti, who graciously allowed me the time to write and provided moral support when I needed it

Above: San Bernardo was settled around 850 AD by ancestors of the Pedretti and Cerletti families who are featured characters in our epic. The original settlers chose to live in this remote and inaccessible spot in order to avoid war, violence and thievery. While they probably did not know it, by isolating themselves from the rest of Europe, they also reduced the odds that they would be victims of plagues that ravished Europe about three times every century. Life for the Pedrettis changed little for a thousand years until three brothers opted to immigrate to Genoa, Wisconsin in 1854.

Below: Campodolcino was the home of the Vener, Starlochi, Buzzetti, Zaboglio and Della Morte families who also play major roles in our epic. –Photo by Luigi Fanetti

The Story of Our Stories

An epic told in twelve volumes

Time to Journey Home—Read about the author's journey to discover an epic tale that defined who we are and that helps us find a moral compass.

The Veneid—Meet our mothers, going back to Mitochondrial Eve.

Begetters of Children—Track our epic family from 840 to 1951.

Lost Book of Maria Prima della Morte—Listen to a mother who was strong before her time (1758–1817).

L'Ultima Preghiera—Relive Teresa Cerletti's life (1805–1853) on the San Bernardo mountainside through her final prayer.

Lettere d'Amore—Join Stefano and Adelaide's love journey to the new world (1853–1855).

The Diary of an Immigrnt: Giovanni Vener—Discover an immigrant's life and insights by reading his private diary (1899).

Peter, a Profile—Meet the transitional master planter (1861–1951).

The Book of Agnes—Follow the deeds of one of Walt Whitman's "unknown heroes equal to the greatest heroes known!" (1922–1963).

Hoe-ers—Remember the good old days, told by twelve participants (1924–1995).

Mick, Memoirs of a Planter—Plan and plant with the author, from seeding cornfields and milking cows to making theater to producing international theater festivals to writing this epic.

Il Lavoro di Artisti—Delight in the visual imagination of the children of the children of Agnes.

Contents

I celebrate myself, and sing myself,

And what I assume you shall assume,
For every atom belonging to me as good belongs to you.

- Opening lines from "Song of Myself" by Walt Whitman

Preface to the Series

It is possible that as many as 115 billion people were born before us. But you and I have each had more than one hundred billion ancestors since the first settlers arrived on the eastern side of the Mount of San Bernardo overlooking the Valley of San Giacomo in Sondrio, Lombardy, Italy, around 840 AD. If you trace our ancestry back to the time of Caesar, each of us would have to identify more than 288 quadrillion grandparents or 288 million billion ancestors. If you would like to fill out your family chart dating back to the mythological Eve born around 4,004 BC, you would have to identify seven times as many people, or 1.6 to the 57th power. What if we go back to the year of Lucy?

You get the idea. There is no way, with that many ancestors, that you and I do not share a few billion of the same grandparents, making us not double cousins, not even cousins tens of thousands of times, but cousins more than a billion times over. Our genes are so intertwined that we are closer than brothers, closer than sisters, maybe even as close as twins. Yes, you and I, we are cousins—we are of the genes of Mitochondrial Eve, and we share the same genes of billions of her children.

The Story of Our Stories is our story. These tales are as much your tales as they are mine. We have lived them together, we are living them together, we will live them together. We are not only twins, you and I; we are joined at the heart. To quote Walt Whitman, "Every atom belonging to me as good belongs to you."

Introduction

"I sing of arms and man"
—Virgil, *The Aeneid*

"I sing of kindness and woman"
—Pedretti, *The Story of Our Stories*

The mandate for an epic is to identify and celebrate who the people are and what their potential is. In Homer's and Virgil's eras, the epic hero was a male warrior whose violent behavior led to victories that inspired loyalty, patriotism, and submission to the ruling class. "I sing of arms and man," is the opening line of Virgil's poem about a brutal warrior who begets a bellicose Rome and the ancestors of the combatant Caesar Augustus. His epic celebrated empire builders, encouraged retaliation, and downplayed the massive cost of lives, enforced slavery, and legalized classism.

Should the modern epic celebrate dominance, war, and revenge? Will today's epic promote limitation, exclusion, and restriction? Is it not possible to put the historic, gentry-sponsored classism, war, violence, and tribalism into the past? Isn't today's hero the commoner, making things happen by mass commitment rather than individual supremacy—more interested in planting seeds than in accumulating power, in making advancements rather than blowing up people, tradition, and peace—more willing to fight for fair treatment with words than domination by war—more concerned with kindness than control—capable of letting empathy replace revenge? Today's epic hero is a planter: one who plants and cultivates; one who plans and nourishes. Our hero has no power or desire to raid the work of others. Our hero cannot come from the privileged class— by definition a people who rely on other's plantings to harvest their successes. Our story is not the story—cannot be the story—of someone indulging in the unjust wealth born of another's labor. No, our story is hidden in the mothers, "who long since left the shores of craving, supremacy and war to explore generosity, affection, and creativity." Come; join me in play, kindness, and song.

> I sing of kindness and of woman
> Serf no more, never Lord
> And of the suffering they endured
> Trodden under the might of the Sons of Misogyny
> Those ministers of misery who maltreated our mothers
> Turning brother against sister, husband against wife,
> Parent against child, mother against mother.
> Tell me, reader, how it all began, why so much spite?
> What did our mothers do to deserve their vengeance?

In *The Aeneid*, Virgil celebrated the Roman conqueror; I celebrate the planter of seeds. Virgil celebrated war; I celebrate harmony. Virgil celebrated dominance; I celebrate parity. Virgil praised father Augustus; I praise mother Eve.

The Story of Our Stories is the story of Marianna and Petronella, Peter and John, Adelaide and Stefano, and

Agnes and her children. It is about the individuals who peopled the Mount of San Bernardo and who turned the roughness of Bad Ax, Wisconsin into the gentleness of Genoa, but first and foremost it is our story, the story of you and me. Our story is written as an epic composed of twelve books, each with a supportive appendix. Each book covers a different story. Some cover the life of a typical family member of a specific generation; others reflect many people of a generation; another traces the entire story from beginning to now; and one looks into a future predicated by the behavior of our mothers. Each volume tells a critical part of the story, is an integral part of the whole, and plays into the unfolding of the epic. While part of a whole, each book can be read independent of the rest.

San Rocco

A sub-division of San Bernardo
Home of the Pedretti family for over 300 years

THE STORY OF OUR STORIES

BOOK I

Time to Journey Home

"The Journey is my home. . . . The universe is made of stories, not of atoms."
—Muriel Rukeyser

"Your descendants shall gather your fruits."
—Virgil

April 17, 2009

The time was now. The call was strong. It was time to journey home. Not home to Genoa, Wisconsin, where I was born and raised, but to that home on the mountain of San Bernardo and in the nearby valley town of Campodolcino where so many of my ancestors had lived for centuries, before circumstances uprooted them from their traditions and forced them west to the untested wilderness of western Wisconsin 150 years ago. It was a journey that led to finding out about long-lost ancestors and new facts about known ancestors. But that was not the call I heard. The need was simpler and more profound than collecting facts. I had to stand where my forebears stood, walk the streets they had walked, watch the same sunset over the same mountain with my girlfriend in my arms, stand on the very spot where a great-great-great-grandfather wooed the love of his life, worship where they worshipped, maybe even drink an espresso at the same bar. I invite you to come on that journey with me now to experience the connection and maybe even re-root yourself on firmer ground.

I grew up, like many other Americans, with little knowledge of anything before myself. Maybe I knew even less than most. As the twelfth child, I never heard the stories of my dad or mom's youth, about how mean my grandparents were or how brave and generous my great-grandparents were. Maybe they had told those stories so many times to their older children they thought we were all sick of hearing about them, so they turned silent about the past.

Or possibly they knew very little themselves. Consider this: My mother's mother, Mary Caroline Nicolatti, was born in Italy. She had nine children and more than fifty grandchildren. She was still alive to attend the weddings of some of her grandchildren. Yet not one of her children or grandchildren knew where she had been born in Italy, and at some point someone made up the story she had been born in Trieste. Not until 2011, some fifty-five years after her death, did we discover she had been born in Trento. The story was that her mother was born in Austria, and her father born in Italy. In fact, both were born in towns near Trento. All of Grandmother's children and many of her grandchildren knew her parents. Still, I repeat, not one knew where they were born and raised.

How soon they forgot. It is hard to believe they did not make a conscious effort to forget, as if the world of their parents and grandparents would somehow contaminate the new world of lusciousness they found in the deep, rich, black soil (tended for millennia by natives) and turn the fertile dirt into the barren and overused and abused land they had left behind. Consider further, my parents not only did not know where their grandparents came from, but they had no idea that three of them, who came from the same narrow, ten-mile-long valley in Northern Italy called Valle San Giacomo (Saint James Valley, defined on the south by Chiavenna and on the other sides by mountains rising three thousand feet above sea level) almost certainly knew each other back in the old country.

I recall knowing only two things: one, that my dad's grandfather, Stefano Pedretti, came from a place called Saint Bernard, Italy (but Dad had no idea where that might be), because that was what was carved on Stefano's gravestone in the Saint Charles Cemetery in Genoa; the other was that I thought I had more Austrian blood in me than Italian, but that turned out not to be true.

There is a reason that families throughout history, and in every country, pass on their stories from generation to generation. These stories become part of who we are and assist us in finding a moral compass. Luckily, I had discovered the power of literature as a teenager, so I had a substitute for my own personal family's stories. But a substitute is still a substitute. Little by little I became aware of an elemental need to know the real stories, to fill this void in my life.

In 1990 I was invited to be a guest at the International Festival of Mime in southern France, and I decided to take the opportunity to add on a honeymoon in Florence and Venice. It was considerably more economical to fly to Paris and rent a car than it was to fly to Milan. Nancy Hill, my bride, and I decided to drive through Switzerland, and I chose to route our trip to cross from Switzerland into Italy at the famous Great Saint Bernard Pass, best known for its dogs. Maybe that was the birthplace of my dad's grandfather, Stephen Pedretti. It wasn't. Still, during the night, sleeping in a loft room of a rustic hotel just past the Swiss-Italian border, I had a dream about the most ordinary woman of all times, who was, on second look, an extraordinary woman. Upon waking in the middle of the night, I realized the person I dreamt about was a blend of my mother, Agnes Venner, and her two sisters, who had also married sons of Peter Pedretti. I began to write furiously about the heroine of my dream. By the time Nancy awoke I had the first three chapters of a novel written, and I dashed off the fourth before we headed down the mountain. I completed the first draft of the book in two months and then put the draft aside.

A decade or so later I got my hands on three manuscripts that deeply inspired me because they included names, dates, events, and some fables about my family's roots that I had no idea anybody knew or cared about. Jim Venner, my double first cousin and the son of Francis Venner and Mary Margaret Pedretti, had spent years building a manuscript, *From Campodolcino to Genoa, the Descendants of Francesco Zaboglio*, that identified fifty-nine of our ancestors, going back in one family to Antonio Buzzetti, who was born in 1569. It was a massive undertaking and had been researched with meticulous care. The edition I received was published in 1996. Shortly thereafter I was told that Jean Pedretti-Flottmeyer, also a double first cousin and the daughter of Albert Pedretti and Helen Venner, had made a manuscript simply called *Malin*, tracing the roots of Grandpa Peter's wife and our grandmother Margaret "Maggie" Malin-Pedretti. *Malin* was another labor of love, filled with seventy-one pages of the descendants of my great-great-grandfather Josef Anton Malin (born August 16, 1847), covering 149 years right up to and past the birth of my daughter Victoria, who was born in March 1995. The book included wedding pictures of my parents, all my aunts and uncles and Grandpa Peter Pedretti, along with pictures of Grandma Maggie's parents. At about the same time, I purchased a copy of *Tracing Our Roots* by Susanne Pedretti, the daughter of Joseph Pedretti, the son of Stephen, whose father was my great-grandfather Stefano Pedretti. Susanne had traveled via a circuitous route back to San Bernardo, a small village overlooking Chiavenna, Sondrio, Italy, on the mountain side of Valle San Giacomo. With the help of a couple of local citizens she found proof that this was indeed the Saint Bernard where Stefano Pedretti was born and spent the first twenty-seven years of his life before immigrating in 1854 to Bad Ax City, which a few years later became Genoa, Wisconsin.

These manuscripts motivated me to make a graphic representation of my genealogical past. As I developed that work for myself, I decided a modified version of the pictograph booklet would be of interest to my children and to my brothers and sisters, so I made seventeen versions and gave them as holiday presents in 2002. That was my project for that year. I have been studying a new topic or taking on a new project each year for the past couple of decades. In 2009 I decided it was time to discover my family's story—to explore my own roots. I would make my annual study for 2009 the area of Italy where my ancestors once lived. A little research informed me that Italy was divided into twenty regions, and that Campodolcino, Vho, San Bernardo, San Giacomo Filippo, Como, Sondrio, and a few other places referenced as "towns of origins" of both the Pedretti and Venner families were in a northernmost region called Lombardy. Thus began my study.

I learned that the specific area the Pedretti and Venner families came from was called Valle San Giacomo. I looked up the area on Google Earth, found websites with photographs and detailed stories about the communities, devoured every book I could find on the region, reread the Venner, Flottmeyer, and Pedretti books, and referred time and again to my graphic representation to see which ancestor was alive during the period I was studying. Soon I felt a powerful need to return. I had to go! And I had to go now. I wanted to make the most of my trip "home," so I immediately contacted the mayor of Campodolcino, who put me in touch with the director of tourism for the area. Then I called Jim Venner. Both suggested I contact two of the foremost experts on the area, Luigi Fanetti and Paulo Via, who were deeply invested in local history, genealogy, and the connection between Genoa, Wisconsin, and Campodolcino. As I spoke no Italian, I would need an interpreter if I was going to carry on conversations with the people I hoped to meet, so I called my friend Anne Guerrieri, who lives in Rome, to inquire if she would be available. She spoke perfect Italian, French, and English, and had told me in detail about her own voyage home, to Georgia, where her ancestors were of the ruling class before

Stalin cut them down. She immediately understood why I needed to do this and enthusiastically offered to serve as interpreter and fellow researcher in Valle San Giacomo, and to make calls for me when I needed someone to speak Italian or French as I prepared for the trip.

One contact led to another, and soon I was picking the brains of Bill Trussoni in Genoa, Jean Pedretti-Flottmeyer in La Crosse, Susanne Pedretti in Cincinnati, Jim Venner in Denver, Malinda Jankord-Steedman in Seattle, Tony Buzzetti in South Carolina, Enrica Guanella, the curator of the Campodolcino museum, and Carl Francoli in Australia. In addition to valuable information and invaluable suggestions, all these people gave me links to websites of interest. Everyone seemed excited about my trip, giving me advice on where to visit, whom to meet and where to stay. Luigi Fanetti offered to prepare a genealogical chart tracing back the ancestors of Stefano Pedretti, Giovanni Venner, and Mary Madeline Sterlocchi, pivotal members of the three families in my ancestry that had emigrated from Val San Giacomo to Genoa. Paulo Via offered to host us and to provide invaluable historical context to my studies. He also introduced me to his daughter, who taught English as a second language and who would prove to be a vital link to the past for me. I was on the phone at least once a week with Annie Guerrieri, who made calls for me to gather information from tourist agencies, archives, museums, and other places where language was a barrier. Annie was a renowned international theater producer, and her networking skills surfaced on my behalf. Every time we talked, she had new information or new contacts for me. I discovered that Annie's last name, Guerrieri, translated to

"The Warrior," and clearly she was living up to her name, never hesitating to take the lead in finding new information or sources to make my journey home a meaningful experience. I pored over maps and memorized the names and locations of the nine communities that make up Campodolcino. I made plans to travel in early August to San Bernardo and Campodolcino.

I wanted to take gifts to the people in Campodolcino who had been so helpful and had shown so much interest in Genoa and my trip. When Luigi Fanetti asked for photos and information about Genoa, I thought that would make the perfect gift. I collected about three dozen pictures and made several copies. I got permission to copy Susanne's book. I also put together a 315-page manuscript that added to Jim Venner's massive research work; a couple dozen pictures, including some old pictures of Genoa that I had found at the Wisconsin Historical Society; and land plots of past history. In the process of making this gift, I learned and relearned what a rich history there was in Genoa, my family, and my roots.

It seemed I had barely had time to pack before it was July 28 and we were boarding the plane in Newark, New Jersey, on our way to Milan, the capital of Lombardy. We spent a couple of days in Milan enjoying saffron risotto much like Mother made and an air-dried beef (called bresaola) that was nearly as good as my dad made. We visited the Duomo in Milan, where Charles Borromeo was once Cardinal and where his body still rests. It seems he came from a very rich and powerful family and was an extremely conservative leader. Saint Charles, the church in Genoa, Wisconsin, where I had attended daily Mass when I was an elementary student, was named after Cardinal Charles Borromeo. The connection between my birthplace and Lombardy was being made for me. Nancy and I took the train to Venice, and our second honeymoon was even lovelier than our first.

St. Charles Cemetery, Genoa, Wisconsin

NATIVE OF
ST. BARNARD, ITALY
DIED
APRIL 1, 1869
AGED 43 YEARS
He left a wife and five children

August 6, 2009: Thursday

We left Venice around eleven a.m. and drove to Lecco, where we had arranged to meet our friend Annie "The Warrior" Guerrieri, who was taking the train from Rome to serve both as our front person and as interpreter for my journey back to Valle San Giacomo. Lecco is a small town on the southeast corner of Lake Como and is less than one and a half hours from Campodolcino.

I was determined to make my first stop in Valle San Giacomo at the Santuario Madonna di Gallivaggio,[1] the famous church containing the rock upon which two young peasant girls who were collecting chestnuts professed they saw Mary, the Mother of Jesus, appear in 1492 to warn them, "If the sinners do not convert, the world will not last long." For centuries worshippers had come here to kiss the rock and to be healed of this or that ailment. I was not so much interested in getting healed by the powers of the Rock, placed front and center in this striking building, as I was excited about being in the space where I had just weeks before learned that my great-great-grandparents, Bartholomew Sterlocchi and Marianna Zaboglio, had exchanged vows on March 5, 1847. This was just eight years before they would boldly, with their two small children, set out for a faraway place with the less-than-inviting name of Bad Ax City, the central municipality of Bad Ax Township on the far western edge of Bad Ax County in the brand-new state of Wisconsin in the United States of America. All

---

[1] Literally translated, this would be the Sanctuary of the Madonna of Gallivaggio. A more accurate translation might be the Mother of Mercy of Gallivaggio.

these Bad Ax locations took their name from Bad Ax River—spelled variously as Bad Axe or Badax—which ran through the county and township just south of the city and was known primarily as the place where white settlers had massacred the children and women who had been following the Native American warrior Black Hawk as they were trying desperately to escape across the Mississippi River.

A few years later Marianna's brother, John Zaboglio, immigrated to Genoa with their mother and my great-great-great-grandmother, Teresa Buzzetti-Zaboglio. As Grandmother Teresa is my only ancestor born in the eighteenth century to immigrate to the United States, I think of her as the earliest immigrant in our shared ancestry to arrive in America, even though at least six of our ancestors were already settled in Genoa when she arrived, including her granddaughter, Mary Madeline, who would become my great-grandmother. I fantasized that Mary Madeline was the first in that family to place her little foot on land. It didn't take much for me to jump from that data to believe that the immigration process began on the day Bart and Marianna exchanged vows in this church and pledged to begin a new life together. Like so many others, Bartholomew and Marianna may have decided, after the failed revolution of 1848, to strike out for America; but for a romantic like me it is more fun to believe that Marianna agreed to marry Bart only when he promised to take her and her mother to the Promised Land.

Nancy and I walked up the steep entrance of about fifty steps that, over the past five hundred years, thousands of the sick had crawled up on their bellies to be healed. We walked into a Mass being said by the parish priest. Perfect. I sat down and took in the architecture, then let my imagination run free. I pictured Marianna walking ever so slowly up the aisle toward her groom, Bartholomew Sterlocchi. Marianna had lost her father shortly after she turned twelve years old. With three much younger siblings, including her youngest brother barely two months old, Marianna, the eldest daughter, and her older brother, Agostino, became head of the household. Now that the youngest had turned twelve, she felt comfortable accepting Bart's proposal and looked forward to having someone take care of her for a change. She was dressed in tasteful, elegant, traditional wedding black, beaming with hope for a rich future. Bart stood waiting: solid, strong, ready to take on the world. The bells tolled to announce to the village that the ceremony was about to begin.

My reverie passed, and I knew it was time to get on the road. I had told Paolo Via and Luigi Fanetti that I planned to arrive in Campodolcino around six p.m., and it was already a few minutes past six. I did not feel rushed, as I had no plans to meet them until later that evening, but I wanted to arrive and get settled in.

As we drove up to Ca' de Val hotel, Paolo Via was waiting for us in the parking lot of Saint John the Baptist, whose lot, I would discover, the hotel used for their guests' cars. Paolo welcomed us warmly, asked about the trip, and informed us that Luigi Fanetti would show us around the next day. We arranged a time and place to meet with Paolo on Saturday, the day following, as he informed me that he needed to get back to Chiavenna for a prior commitment. Before he could leave, Luigi Fanetti and Dino Buzzetti arrived, and Paolo introduced us. They welcomed Nancy and me with genuine enthusiasm and warmth. Annie could hardly keep up with the translation, as they were bubbling with excitement that they had been more successful than they had hoped in their efforts to identify my ancestry. Later, when I studied the documents they had prepared, I would discover just how successful they had been. Included were more than sixty-five new names of ancestors, more than doubling the number of ancestors identified in Jim Venner's book. They had put enormous effort into this research, and the results proved they were extremely good at tracing ancestral paths. After arranging to meet the next morning at nine o'clock, Luigi and Dino gave me a multipage chart of my ancestry. I wanted to study the document, but I was too exhausted from the day, which had begun in Venice eighteen hours earlier. I lay down, and the next thing I knew it was six a.m., time to organize for the new day and get some breakfast.

Steps to
Santuario Madonna di Gallivaggio

It is believed by many that the Virgin Mary appeared to two young girls on October 10, 1492 and that she stood on the rock that is located inside the Sanctuary of Mary of Gallivaggio, Mother of Mercy

Many ancestors of Giovanni Venner and Mary Madeline Starlochi were married in this chapel.

Photo by Luigi Fanetti

Santuario Madonna di Gallivaggio
Author near the top of the steps with cemetery and
tower in back ground.

August 6, 2009
Photo by Nancy B Hill

Santuario Madonna di Gallivaggio

Santuario Madonna di Gallivaggio
Interior
Photos by Luigi Fanetti

Marianna Zabolio & Bartholomew Starlochi were married in Santuario Madonna di Gallivaggio on 5 March 1847. Above photo likely taken on one of their anniversaries. Below is a photo of Mr. Starlochi taken after they moved to Aberdeen, South Dakota.

Maria Teresa Dominica Petronella Buzetti-Zaboglio was the mother of Mrs. Marianna Zabolio-Starlochi. She is seen here posing with her son Giovanni Battista, near the time they immigrated to Genoa. She was the first owner of the 40 acres of section 28 where the St. Charles Cemetery is located. It is believed that she donated the land to the Catholic Church.

Photo taken in 1850s

St. John the Baptist Church
Via Tini
Campodolcino, Lombardia 23021
Italy

We met Paulo Via in this parking lot.

The Old Roman Bridge, Campodolcino's most famous historical sight
Photo Luigi Fanetti

Campodolcino, Sondrio, Lombardy. Italy
Photo taken from Old Roman Bridge

The author, Nancy Hill and Paulo Via
August 2009

August 7, 2009: Friday

After breakfast I could have studied the genealogical chart, but I decided I wanted to walk up to the old Roman Bridge, Campodolcino's most famous historical sight. There would be time to study the chart later—if not while I was here, then when I got back home. Annie, Nancy, and I walked up to the bridge and took in the vista. There were some *oohs* and *aahs*, followed by comments to each other of how fantastic this was. After a few moments to take it in and allow the place to heal me, it was time to meet Luigi Fanetti and Dino Buzzetti.

Luigi came by the hotel at nine a.m., and I gave him copies of all the photos that I had printed and an up-to-date ahnentafel version of Jim Venner's *From Campodolcino to Genoa, the Descendants of Francisco Zaboglio*, which I had printed and bound just days before. Fortunately, I had made an extra copy, and when we picked up Dino Buzzetti in San Giacomo on the way to San Bernardo, I was able to give him a copy of the same documents.

Luigi drove us up the narrow, multi-hairpin road to San Bernardo. Driving up the mountain, Annie was busy every second translating, as Luigi and Dino spoke with enthusiasm about their findings and about the area and its history. I found that electroshock therapy was first used and popularized by Ugo Cerletti, a distant relative, whose family came from San Bernardo. Dino joked this may not be something I wanted to brag about. Luigi told me he and Dino had spent hours in San Bernardo and had found numerous documents identifying my ancestors in the church records, and that they would show the manuscripts to me. As we drove through Olmo, a village about a fifteen-minute walk from San Bernardo, I was told that people from Olmo felt superior to those from San Bernardo, and to this day they will say something like "You must be from San Bernardo" if someone acts stupidly. It seemed foolish to have rivalry between two tiny towns close together but isolated from the rest of the world.

As we came into San Bernardo my eyes darted everywhere. I was trying to take it all in at once, to make it mine. I got out of the car and took a deep breath to inhale the pure mountain air Great-Grandpa Stefano Pedretti had breathed 150 years earlier. I glanced over the top of the car and down into the valley below, where Chiavenna seemed asleep at the junction of Valle San Giacomo, Val Bregaglia, and Val Bodengo. My eyes began to rove up the mountain behind the city. I noticed Luigi and Dino were enthusiastically greeting a tall, distinctive-looking man. They immediately came my way and introduced me to Alberto Cerletti, who told me he had lived in San Bernardo and that he was a distant relative. Later I found out that he was the person whom Susanne Pedretti had met in San Bernardo in 1996. He had searched through the records for Susanne and found the documents that had proven this was the Saint Bernard where Stefano Pedretti had been born and raised before emigrating. They found information about Stefano's birth, marriage, and death, along with similar information about ten of his siblings and his parents, Guglielmo Pedretti and Maria Teresa Cerletti, whose information included the names of Stefano's grandparents. I was informed that Alberto, Luigi, and Dino, while searching through the records in anticipation of my arrival had found a list of four other of Stefano's siblings and several additional ancestors going back three more generations.

Before I had the opportunity to feel or express my amazement, they told me they had identified some ruins where my ancestors had once lived, and they would take me there before we returned to Campodolcino. That's what I had come for; I was ready to head there first. I wanted to stand on the ancestral ground where my foreparents ate, slept, and huddled in front of the family fireplace on a cold winter night. Luigi pointed behind me, where an old cistern was still running and had a date of 1710 on it, indicating that it had been serving the village since then and that at least six generations of my grandparents drank water from this very fountain! I went to touch it, to drink a handful of water from its spout, to photograph it in order to bring this moment back to my home in America. We walked onto the San Bernardo churchyard, took in again the magnificent view of Chiavenna below and the surrounding mountains popping up in every direction, and studied a memorial to soldiers killed in action in the two world wars. Surnames of those memorialized included men from the Cerletti, Lombardini, de Stefani, and Gadola families, all names identified as ancestors.

We went into the church, took many pictures, and went upstairs to look at the historical tablets identifying births, baptisms, weddings, and deaths of the citizens of San Bernardo. I was shown several pages recording my ancestors, and I was able to photograph seven of them. Luigi would later give me photographs of eight more pages from these documents, providing me with pictures of fifteen primary documents that chronicled my family, and Alberto Cerletti added even more and provided most of the translations found in the appendixes. While there, Alberto, Luigi, and Dino found some records identifying additional ancestors. They asked me to give them my ancestry chart so they could add the new information.

Before I knew it, I was told we had to leave because my hosts had an important engagement to attend. We had been on the mountain for close to two hours, but it felt like ten minutes to me. I had not yet had a moment to connect with my ancestors, or even to just be alone long enough to let the space enter my being. To me, this was the primary reason to go anyplace. I had not let that happen because I had assumed I would have that opportunity later in the day.

We started down the mountain. Luigi stopped to let me take in and photograph the panoramic view of San Bernardo. It was one of those moments when sadness and joy collide. As I looked back at San Bernardo, snuggled into the ravine, I thought to myself, "You have just spent two hours in the mysterious and legendary San Bernardo of your youth. You walked on the same church lawn as your great-grandfather Stefano Pedretti, saw the stunning view your great great-grandma Maria Teresa Cerletti loved, walked through the doors and down the aisle that so many of your great-grandmothers had walked, to wed or to baptize their newborn. You held in your hands records dating back to the early sixteen hundreds that recorded the roots of the Pedretti family. You met and chatted with Alberto Cerletti and his two utterly charming grandchildren. You've just experienced one of the greatest thrills in your life." My awe collided and blended with a deep disappointment at having to leave this all behind after too short a stay.

Luigi took a left turn off the road to Campodolcino and explained that he was taking us to Vho, the original home of the Buzzetti family, where my great-great-great-grandma Teresa Buzzetti was born and lived until she married Francesco Zaboglio, who was from the Campodolcino frazione (outlying village) of Starleggia on the other side of the town. Luigi told us to take our time walking around the village. I continued to be surprised at how small these villages had remained and how every building here looked like it must have for centuries. I had no trouble believing that I was looking at the same view that Francesco Zaboglio would have seen when he came courting Maria Teresa Buzzetti in 1820. We came around the second house and saw a housekeeper washing her clothes by hand in the village trough. I thought if I'd been here 180 years ago, I might be looking at Maria Teresa or her mother. The sidewalk took us to the front door of San Antonio Church. I was deeply disappointed to find the church doors locked.

Vho sat at the edge of the valley, snuggled into the mountainside as if it belonged there—as if it had always been there even before man, "the shining brow" of the valley. Frank Lloyd Wright would have loved the way this town blended into its natural setting, seeming to grow out of the place where valley meets mountain rather than interrupting it. The entire village reminded me of Wright's estate Taliesin ("shining brow") in Spring Green, Wisconsin. I fell in love with the place, although I am not so sure I could live there.

Luigi dropped us off at our hotel, Ca' de Val in Campodolcino, for lunch. We decided we would rather walk around and find a different place to eat. On the way to lunch we stopped at Scaramella's deli and picked up some bresaola to snack on. I wanted it to taste even closer to my memory of my father and mother's dried beef than what I had tasted in Milan, but it did not. Still, it was delicious. We found La Cantina, a trattoria owned by Roberto Guanella. I don't recall any signage, and the only thing that indicated it was a restaurant was an open stairway that seemed more public than private. We did not find it on our own but were told by the upstairs store owner that the stairs led to a restaurant. The entire inside was stone, the ceilings in both rooms arched. It was as enticing and attractive as a rustic restaurant is allowed to get. The waitress was pleasant, and the food was unexpectedly gourmet. As we were there after the lunch hour, the place was empty, so the chef was happy to come out and charm us with tales of Italian food and restaurants.

After lunch, Luigi picked us up at the hotel and drove us to Ca' Bardassa, a former home turned into a museum of the time that is located in Fraciscio, a frazione of Campodolcino. Fraciscio was the hometown of many families who immigrated to Genoa, Wisconsin, including Curti, Trussoni, Levi, Gilardi, and Guanella. Our guide was Giovanni Trussoni, a name that brought back memories of John Trussoni and his wife, the only two residents of Genoa that I knew as a child who conversed in Italian. Built in the early 1800s, the museum provided an authentic representation of a home during the time my ancestors lived in the area. Even though several of my ancestors had been on the Valle San Giacomo council, I had no reason to believe that any of them would have had the wealth this owner had.

Luigi took us for a scenic drive north toward the Splugen Pass. We stopped at Pianazzo Falls for a stunning view of the valley below. We continued on to an unexpected acre or two of flat land on the side of the mountain where Luigi's daughter, Michela, was supervising a summer youth camp. We then drove to Luigi's house and met his lovely wife, Giuseppina, who served us tea.

I invited Luigi and Giuseppina to join us for dinner the next evening. It seemed the least I could do for all the effort they had put into making my trip one that far exceeded my wildest expectations. They graciously accepted and suggested we eat at La Genzianella in Fraciscio.

Author's first view of San Bernardo
Pedretti home can be seen on hillside just left of steeple
of San Bernardo Church.

For over 700 years Pedretti ancestors were baptized, married and
buried at this church. Photo taken August, 2009

The Parish Church of San Bernardo of San Giacomo district
Spluga Valley
1150

Chiesa Parrocchiale di S. BERNARDO - sopra S. GIACOMO F. - m. 1150 - Valle Spluga

San Bernardo 2009
Chiavenna can be seen in the valley on the left
Photo Luigi Fanetti

Winter, 2009: San Bernardo
Photo by Luigi Fanetti

San Rocco Chapel
Built in the 1630s to honor San Rocco who was credited
with saving San Bernardo from the effects of the Great
Plague of Milan.

Water trough collecting spring water
San Bernardo, 2009

Author in room in San Bernardo Church
where archival records are stored
with Mauro, Anna, and Alberto Cerletti, Dino Buzzetti and Luigi
Fanetti - Photo by Nancy B Hill

Below: Anne Guerrieri and Nancy Hill
At La Cantina, a trattoria owned by Roberto Guanella.

VHO, 2009

August 8, 2009: Saturday

I had a rough night, waking up every thirty minutes or so. About three fifteen I gave up trying to get back to sleep for the sixth time and took out the log I was keeping of our trip. I realized I had not written in it for three days. By five a.m. I had caught up and was finally feeling tired enough to go back to sleep. Back up at seven. We were not planning to eat until eight thirty, so I freshened up and stole out of the room for a solo hike to the old Roman Bridge, which was just up behind the hotel. Built by the Romans in the eighth century, the bridge has provided safe passage from Tini to Corti ever since. Other bridges have been built in modern times, so the bridge is now used for foot passage and occasional ceremonies. This early in the morning, the only sound I heard was the water trickling underneath me. The water came down through a ravine defined by two steep embankments, formed over the centuries by the rush of water. In August the creek was quiet, but I had been told that in the spring it could live up to its name, Torrente Rabbiosa, or Raging River. In 1935 the raging waters flooded the city and caused massive damage, including completely washing away the remains in the cemetery. After that flood the citizens built tall stone embankments to contain the spring floods.

From the bridge I saw a miniature world: valleys, fields, mountains, churches, houses, walkways, people beginning to mill about, a couple of dogs and a cat. Alone on a foggy morning, I had some fun imaging which of my ancestors courted on this bridge. It seemed the obvious place to take your girl and make out. With its charm and history, you

could hardly find a more romantic spot to weaken the
resistance of a young girl living in a culture that frowned on
premarital kissing. I visualized an earlier eighth day of
August; let's say it was 1852, with young Giovanni Vener,
who would become my great-grandfather, rendezvousing
on the very spot I stood with his latest squeeze—maybe
even Angelina Zaboglio, the aunt of Mary Madeline
Starlochi—whom Giovanni would marry some fifteen years
later. I saw Giovanni telling jokes and bragging about this
or that accomplishment. Angelina looked smitten by the
charm and friskiness of Giovanni and flattered that this
handsome boy, three years her senior, was giving all his
attention to please her. In my mind's eye, Giovanni had
earlier in the day arranged to meet Angelina, who would
later immigrate to Genoa and marry Anthony Levi, in the
first recorded marriage in the new Saint Charles Church, in
July 1872. She had heard what a Casanova Giovanni could
be, but she felt safe meeting him in the open where they
could be observed from the village. There he might have
told her he was going to bolt, to catch the coach that her
dad once operated to carry mail south to the coastal town of
Genoa, Italy. At Genoa he would board a ship to America
and then travel to Bad Ax, which, Giovanni Trussoni from
Fraciscio had written back, was teeming with fields of black
dirt waiting to be claimed by a young, ambitious man. He
hinted that he would like to take her with him. In the
shadow of the evening Giovanni turned Angelina so she
was facing him but blocked in view from the village; he
stepped toward her, and they engaged in a passionate kiss.

Above the bridge, the banks of the stream went straight
up. These would be a sure temptation to a young buck

wanting to impress the lady of the hour. I thought, "I bet ole Giovanni scaled that surface when he was trying to prove he was the Catch of the Village." I started to connect to Giovanni, saw him climb the wall off to my right. Watched him maneuver the rock and edge his way to the top. It was that kind of bravery, foolish as it might have been, that could have prepared him to take the carriage route heading south to Milan and on to Genoa to finagle a job on a freighter heading to New Orleans and then crew a steamboat up the Mississippi River to seek land in the Campodolcino colony of Bad Ax, Wisconsin. (Later Ilearned he camc via La Havre).

Whoops! It was after eight thirty; I had to get to breakfast so we could meet Paolo Via in the Chiavenna parking lot behind the Giuriani Lumber Yard at ten o'clock. We left early so we could make this a scenic drive, taking in more of the view than we had on the way in. We also wanted some extra time to find the parking lot. Paolo's directions were clear, but in a strange town with signs in a language we could not always read, we needed to allow that we might get lost. We got there just fine, but we weren't so sure we were there. We were in a parking lot by a lumber yard not too far from the hospital. But was it Giuriani's lumber yard? We could not find a sign. About then Paolo called and assured me that we were in the correct lot. He lived above the lumber yard and quickly came down to meet us. Paulo drove us to the Vertemate Palace, where his daughter Valentina was waiting to greet us.

The palace was a testimony to how wealthy this area of Italy once was. It was surrounded by a spacious and beautiful garden. Inside the palace were large, comfortable rooms, beautifully decorated with carved wood and paintings by gifted artists. The views, looking out extremely large windows from the seventeenth century, were breathtaking. But this was not the palace of a nobleman. It was the home of a merchant of the Vertemate family. In fact, it was the family's summer home. Their primary home, reputed to be four times the size of the Vertemate palace, had once stood across the valley in the village of Piuro, just east of Chiavenna. The citizens of Piuro were successful farmers and craftsmen. They mined the local pot stone and shaped it into cooking pots and vessels that were both works of art and valuable cookware due to the stone's ability to retain heat and cold. Since Piuro sat at a vital fork for trade between the Orient and Switzerland and Germany, the merchants had the means to export their goods. But even more important to the amassing of wealth was the ability to collect tolls from the traders who found it convenient to traverse their roads to carry their goods over the Alps.

The people of Piuro, along with their palaces lining the hillside of the ancient town, were tragically buried in a landslide in the middle of the night of September 4, 1618. The remaining emblem of that wealthy time is the Palazzo Vertemate. It has been beautifully restored and is now a museum operated by the city of Chiavenna. We had a personal tour of the palace by Paulo, one of the foremost experts on the history of the area, and Valentina, a former tour guide. We learned fascinating, inside information about the palace, the times, and the family.

Jumping four hundred years forward and four thousand miles away, I had been a little embarrassed that the people of Genoa, Wisconsin, did not seem to know how to pronounce either "Genoa" or "risotto." When I found out that Paolo was a linguist specializing in dialects of nineteenth-century Italy, I had to ask if the odd pronunciation of "risot" for risotto had any basis in history. Paolo informed me that "risot" (with sot rhyming with rot) was the way locals in Valle San Giacomo pronounced the word in the mid-nineteenth century. I then asked about Genoa, and again, the Wisconsin pronunciation (Ge pronounced *je* as in Jehovah and *noa* like Noah) was also from the local dialect of the time. So the Genoa, Wisconsin, folks weren't just a bunch of ignorant farmers who did not even know how to pronounce the name of their town or their favorite food; they were carrying on a valuable tradition maintaining the correct pronunciation of words from our heritage. As it turns out, it wasn't just a word or two that the Campodolcino descendants had maintained. The people I met in Campodolcino reminded me of those gentle, reserved, kind, compassionate, and religious souls I grew up with in Genoa, Wisconsin. In both communities, people were fiercely independent on the one hand and openly friendly on the other. You could count on their help without asking, and you trusted that your secrets were safe with them. It was not possible to imagine anyone from Genoa or Campodolcino stepping on someone to get ahead. I remember marveling as a child at people who appeared never to have evil or envious thoughts about anyone or anything. I thought the same seemed to be true of the people I met in Campodolcino and San Bernardo.

During our palace visit, Nancy pulled me aside and informed me that she had told Valentina how much I wanted to return to San Bernardo. To my delight, she told me that Valentina had volunteered to take me up the next day. We decided to meet at the lumber yard parking lot at eight thirty the next morning. I wanted to shout "whoopee!" but I stayed calm and merely thanked her about nine times.

While at the palace we learned about the Pietra Ollare pottery that had been so vital to the affluence of the region. We were told that the Ollare stone had been used for centuries to make pots and that my ancestors would have used the Pietra Ollare pots for everyday cooking. Paolo also explained that the stone used to make Pietra Ollare was often translated as soapstone. I asked if it were possible to purchase a pot. Paolo informed me that there was still a family of artists who turned this stone into pots and vessels with a lathe, as had been done for centuries, and that they sold the pots at their factory.

Just past noon, we drove to the factory Lavorazione Pietra Ollare, but it was closed for the traditional Italian siesta time. We would have to return at three p.m. Paolo recommended a restaurant on Pedretti Street (Via Carlo Pedretti) where Nancy and I could eat lunch—Trattoria del Mercato di Monte celli Angela—and graciously walked with us to the restaurant. We found out that Via Carlo Pedretti was named after an important historical person who had led the fight for workers' rights in the second half of the nineteenth century and had been an active supporter of the unification of Italy. While his greatest influence was in Italy, he was also known for his efforts to improve workers' rights in California, where he lived near the end of the century before returning to Chiavenna, where he died in 1909. The city was celebrating the centennial anniversary, but there were no activities during the days we were there. While I know of no direct blood relation to Carlo Pedretti, his parents, Giovanni and Maria Pedretti, were reportedly born in San Bernardo, leaving me no doubt that he was a near relative and acquaintance of my great-grandfather Stefano Pedretti.

Nancy and I wanted to return to the Pietra Ollare, so we had time to kill. We took our time enjoying bresaola, risot, pasta, and some local beer while warmly recollecting our lovely time with the charming and knowledgeable Via family. We both noted how lucky we were that we had been introduced to them prior to arriving here and what wonderful hosts they were. I bubbled over with recounting the past day and a half, expressing many times how excited I was with the information Luigi and Dino had researched. I told Nancy, "This trip is already ten times more meaningful to me than I had dreamed in my wildest fantasies." After lunch we walked from one end of Via Carlo Pedretti to the other. That was about one and a half blocks, which is the typical length of any street in Europe. One end opened into a lively square, and several of the shops were open. We had some time before the soapstone factory was to reopen, so we explored the area. One shop had some appealing artwork and quality pottery. I was tempted to buy two or three items but resisted in favor of purchasing some Pietra Ollare pieces later.

We drove back to the Pietra Ollare factory and storefront and were in for a delightful treat. The place was a virtual museum, showcasing hundreds of pots, vases, cups, and other items. I was taken by the fantastic masks scattered throughout the display area. We were told that once heated, the Ollare stone kept food hot for hours, and that anyone living in the area would have owned one or more. Certainly my great-great-grandmother Teresa Cerletti-Pedretti, who lived in San Bernardo, and Giovanni Venner's mother, Margarita Della Morte, cooked in objects that looked exactly like what I was holding in my hand. I turned the pot with the kind of love and connection my mother used to turn and hold her cast-iron frying pan, which was clearly the favorite object in her kitchen. In her cast-iron pan, she cooked her scrumptious chicken, fried freshly caught sunfish, scrambled eggs, or prepared whatever was the primary dish for our meals. Did she inherit her attachment to a weighty family pot from her great-grandmother Margarita Della Morte?

Margarita suddenly burst into my head. She was standing in her kitchen, plucking the final feathers out of a freshly killed chicken. As she finished, she took out her Ollare frying pot, placed it on the wood stove, tossed in two more pieces of wood, poured some olive oil into the pot, strolled to the pump outside her house to wash the chicken, came back in, dried the chicken, and dropped it into the pot so the oil splattered over the edges. Then she took out a smaller but taller pot, put in some butter, added onions until they were browned, stirred in rice a little at a time until it turned translucent, added small amounts of water while maintaining a boiling temperature, stirred the rice, covered it with a lid, and turned the chicken in the large pot. The movie in my head flashed forward twenty minutes. Margarita was now brewing a saffron tea, which she mixed into the rice before folding cheese into the mixture, re-covering the risot to allow the flavors to blend as she took the chicken out of the Ollare pot, placed it on her cutting board, and elegantly carved it as her family eagerly waited for Sunday dinner. Wait a minute; the scene I was seeing was how my mother prepared Sunday dinner, not in Campodolcino but in Genoa, Wisconsin. Was I superimposing my culture on my great-great-grandmother, who lived in an earlier time in a very different country? No, I think not. Except that she used a cast-iron pot instead of an Ollare pot and folded Wisconsin cheddar into her risot instead of Parmesan cheese, my mother was carrying on a tradition of making a delectable Sunday dinner that was probably part of the Vener–Della Morte–Ghelfi–Buzzetti families for centuries.

Even though I was eager to get back to Campodolcino so I could tour the museum, I could not pull myself away from looking and touching piece after piece. I wondered which piece Teresa might have used, which one Margarita would have inherited. Which one Giovanni would have packed to take to America and then unpacked as he realized how heavy his luggage was? Did anyone bring an Ollare pot to Genoa? If they did, where is it? I wanted the frying pan that looked the shape of my mother's much-used cast-iron pot. But it was much heavier than the cast-iron version and priced well out of my range. The same was true of the masks, which would have made a great addition to my mask collection at home. Best to leave them behind. I had been looking for an adequate gift for Jim Venner, who had been so instrumental in the research about our family and served as my tutor into our past. There was no doubt I was in the right shop for that. I found an elegant wine cup for Jim and picked out a small covered bowl for myself.

We drove back to the hotel. I left Nancy there to get some rest and headed off to meet Enrica Guanella at the Museo della Via Spluga e della Val San Giacomo, a historical museum located in the heart of Campodolcino. Enrica was out when I got there, so I wandered through the museum. I was trying to get a quick overview so that when I came back through the museum with Ms. Guanella at a more leisurely pace, I would have an idea of what to dwell on. I think it is a great way to take in a new place, and I almost always approach a museum or historic sightseeing in this manner. I was on the lookout for the crest of the Pedretti family, which my brother had told me was hanging on the wall. It was not so impressive, but it was of deep interest. There were two scenes. A castle on the mountain made sense. The Pedrettis lived on Mount Saint Bernard and either thought of themselves as of royal stock or, more likely, thought of their home as a castle perched upon a mountaintop, protected from invasion. But what was the ship about? I inquired at the museum and, later, from others, but no one had a theory. Did it represent the later Pedretti clan that took boats to America, or was it an earlier Pedretti clan that came with the Vikings across waters from Denmark or Greenland, or does it represent something more spiritual? For that answer we must wait.

There was a very old list of the council members for the area. On that list I saw many surnames of my ancestral family and families that emigrated from the valley to Genoa, Wisconsin. Among them were Vener, Ghelfi, Levi, Trussoni, Gadola, Della Morte, Buzzetti, and Guanella.

Enrica Guanella arrived, and we went back into the archival area, where she said she had several documents covering activities of Pedrettis that stretched back for centuries. As she was searching for these documents, I mentioned other surnames in my Campodolcino ancestry. When I said Zaboglio, she grabbed a rolled-up scroll she said was an extensive genealogical tree that traced the Zaboglio family back over three hundred years. At first I thought this scroll may have been the source for the data Jim Venner had included in his manuscript, *The Descendants of Francesco Zaboglio*. Ms. Guanella rolled open the scroll and I found my great-great-grandmother Marianna Zaboglio, and we traced back from her to Francesco Zaboglio, the title character of Jim Venner's book. We were only one-third of the way up the page! The hunt was on. We found Francesco's parents, then his grandparents, and slowly but excitedly worked our way up the page and back five more generations to Bartholomew Zaboglio, the progenitor of all the people listed on this scroll. I was instantly somewhere between Nirvana and fainting. With my heart light and giddy and my knees giving in to the thrill of discovery, I worked my way back down the tree one generation at a time, back to Francesco. I concluded I had to be the first person on the hunt for the Pedretti-Venner lineage to peer upon this historic document.

Probably born early in the second half of the sixteenth century, Bartholomew Zaboglio, the family patriarch whose descendants were traced on this document, had fathered Guglielmo, who fathered Giovanni Battista in 1616. Giovanni married Agnese Scaranella in 1656 and had five children before he died in 1684. His son, Agostino married a Gianoli, and they had eleven children. Their tenth child,

Agostino Gabriele, born in 1718, fathered the grandfather of Jim Venner's title character, Francesco Zaboglio.

Now I was ready to see some documents that covered the Pedretti line or other families' stories, but it was already just minutes before six p.m., and the museum was about to close. Nor did I have the time to come back through the museum at a leisurely pace. This museum deserved a couple of days of my time, and I had not managed to spend even a couple of hours. As I left, I promised myself that I would return to Campodolcino soon and plan for a much longer stay.

It was time to return to the hotel and freshen up before we met Luigi and Pino Fanetti for dinner. The restaurant had bresaola made from venison on the menu. I had to try that. It was tasty, but not as good as the beef version. We cracked open a bottle of wine and dined long over conversation, keeping Annie on her toes translating a mile a minute. On the way home, Luigi drove out of the way so we could see Fraciscio at night. The houses and streetlights lit up the valley with magic.

When we got back to the hotel, I crawled into bed and was asleep before my head hit the pillow.

Vertemate Palace
Valentina Via and Nancy B Hill

Via Carlo Pedretti Street
Chiavenna, Sondrio, Lombardy, Italy

Nancy B Hill
proposing a toast on Carlo Pedretti Street

Author
enjoying a local beer at restaurant on Pedretti Street

Bresaola

The author grew up eating dried beef and dried sausage made by his parents. The Bresaola and Bastardèi of Val San Giacomo tastes exactly like that made in Genoa, Wisconsin. There can be no doubt that the Genoa immigrants from Val San Giacomo maintained their ability to make Bresaola (called dried beef in Genoa) and Bastardèi (but using smaller pork casings ala Cacciatorini and called dried sausage in Genoa).

Display of ollare pots
Lavorazione Pietra Ollare Factory
Chiavenna, Sondrio, Lombardy

Hand painted version of Pedretti crest
hanging on a wall in
Museum della Via Spluga e della Val San Giacomo
Campodolcino, Sondrio, Lombardy

August 9, 2009: Sunday

It was Sunday. We would be leaving for Lake Como before the sun set, and this last day was full of plans. Aware of how little time I had left, I relied on my guardian angel to wake me early. I wanted to have the quiet necessary to reflect on what it was like to live here, to sense both the serenity and isolation that so many generations of my ancestors must have experienced. Most of all, I wanted to visit Prestone, the southernmost subdivision of Campodolcino. I had found out since arriving in Campodolcino that Prestone had been the home of my mother's family, the Veners (also spelled Venner), and that they had lived here for many centuries. Could I find in Prestone the origin of what made her the woman who had so shaped my life?

I also thought about revisiting the old Roman Bridge, where the day before I had come close to feeling how a maturing boy of 150 years ago might have felt. I wanted to return, to bond with the young Giovanni Vener, maybe even engage him in a conversation, but I knew if I missed this chance to get to "Venerville"—my newly invented pet name for Prestone—I might not have the chance to sense the secret stories the old houses knew. Maybe, just maybe, I would find in "Venerville" some kernel of truth, an image, an insight, a vision, to inspire me to complete *The Book of Agnes*, the novel I had begun nineteen years earlier about a bountiful mother whose grandfather was from the Vener family of Campodolcino.

I snuck out of the hotel around five thirty a.m., slipped into my car, and eased out of the parking lot. There was neither car nor human in sight, so I drove slowly toward "Venerville" taking in what great-grandpa Giovanni Vener might have seen as he snuck home just before dawn after romancing on the Roman Bridge early on a foggy August morning. I crawled along as slowly as our rental Volkswagen would carry me. At this time of the morning, I imagined that Giovanni would have been walking as fast as possible to get home before his dad, Primo, woke up and whipped his butt good for carousing all night with his latest crush. He was young and strolled in a world waiting to burst with creative energy and revolutions that were seeking life, liberty, and the pursuit of happiness; I was definitely past my prime, traveling by motor car in a world of wars, genocide, and fear, scorched by greed and consumerism. Still, we were taking the same road home searching for meaning, aware of the past, and naively optimistic about the possibilities.

I let the car almost stall in first gear as the downhill grade turned ever so slightly up as the three of us— Giovanni, the VW Rabbit, and I—coasted into "Venerville." I let Giovanni out, and he scooted up a side road to home as I continued on through the town, looking for a place to park so I could step onto the pavement that my mother's grandfather would have tried to wear out courting a Zaboglio, Fanetti, Levi, or Francoli, and going to meet his cousins and buddies in Guanella Tavern.

I drove through town, came to the "You are leaving Campodolcino" sign, pulled into the only side street, backed out onto the S.S. 36 highway, and saw the first car of the day heading directly toward me at top speed. He screeched to a stop and let me go ahead. I sped back through town to avoid further impeding the kind man behind that wheel, who seemed in a hurry to get someplace at five forty-five on a Sunday morning. I pulled into the first parking space and took a few deep breaths, attempting to recapture the calm and the revelations of the morning. After a few minutes passed, I opened the car door and reached back (somewhat from habit and somewhat reluctantly) to grab my camera. I knew I would need pictures to help me remember—not only the shape of the houses, but the thoughts and feelings that were about to own me. At the same time, I knew the camera would act as an obstacle, preventing me from feeling as deeply as I might. The nearly full moon, just starting to wane, was setting over the westernmost mountain as the sky behind began to lighten with the morning sun. I paused and let the moon redirect me. I sensed Giovanni near me and chuckled as I imagined he'd gotten home, ruffled his bed to make Primo think he'd spent the night there, and hurried back to join me.

There was no car or pedestrian to be seen or heard in any direction. The sense of power I felt standing in Grandpa Giovanni Venner's street instantly sent a warm rush through my veins and overpowered my resistance. I enjoyed that feeling possessing me for a few moments, then took out my camera to permanently catch the setting moon before it dropped behind Pizzo Truzzo, a mountain just west of Campodolcino where the Pedrettis once grazed their livestock in the summer. I looked up the street toward the north through worn, gray row homes, and I could not help thinking, "Venerville is one drab place." It made no difference, because it was mine; it was what shaped me and my family. Drab or not, I was taken by the vigor of the cool morning, the confidence of time, the absence of hustle in the scene before me. I sensed Giovanni was punchy, scared, bored, and desperate. He wanted out; I wanted in. I wanted very much to connect with Giovanni, maybe even crawl inside his skin. I decided to engage him in a conversation.

I told him he was about to get out of Prestone. "No way." He would come to America and, in about fourteen years, marry Bart Sterlocchi's daughter, who was now barely two years old. "That's disgusting." He would take over the Sterlocchi farm just outside of Bad Ax, Wisconsin, and turn it into a model farm. "Of course." Within a year of his young wife's death, and three years before his first grandchild was born, he would die in an asylum. Before he had time to turn morose, I told him that grandchild would grow up to become my mother. "Tell me about her."

"She was born in April 1903 to your son Bartholomew, who married a woman from Trento. They christened her Agnes to remind them how pure she looked at birth. She grew up a dutiful daughter and longed foremost to be a nun, but instead she married one of Stefano Pedretti's grandsons. By the time she was sixty she had given life to eighty offspring—fifteen children, sixty-two grandchildren, and three great-grandchildren."

I looked Giovanni right in the eye and said, "Tell me your story, the story of your father and mother and the story of their mothers and fathers." He looked back but said nothing. I continued, "What is in your family, in this town that made the Venner women in my life so extraordinary?"

"My grandmother."

"Go on."

"She was born in 1758, married my grandpa before she turned twenty, and gave birth to eleven children and died before she turned sixty. Didn't you read my book? It is about her."

"What book?"

"The one I'm writing. I started it three months ago. For now, I am calling it *Val San Maria Prima*."

"Go on."

"It begins with her wedding in the Gallivaggio church. If I say so myself, I have a fantastic description of the church and the wedding. Then it goes back to her religious youth, tells how the local priest made advances that scared her away from a convent life, and how her depression led her to rely on a young buck named Primo. I describe her giving birth in our living room to my oldest uncle, Giovanni Primo, and how she dealt with his death two days later. Sound boring? It's not, for I take you inside her mind and soul to tell her story through her eyes and emotions. I tell how she led the recovery of the village following the flood of 1817, spearheaded the efforts to have the Immaculate Conception chapel built, and led the local resistance that ousted the Austrians three years ago—sure they are back, but they treat us a lot better now. I just started to write about the Resistance this morning."

"Did your grandma do all those things? How come I haven't heard about it? Wait a minute; she wasn't even alive during the Resistance."

"She was not," Giovanni admitted. "She did not do all those things, but she could have. I have to tell her story— the story of who she was, not what she was limited to. Born in another time and place, she would ..." His voice trailed off. "She was strong, and I want the reader to know her—her strength and courage modified by her gentle and kind soul. I'm writing a novel, not a biography."

Abruptly he asked me, "Does it become the great novel I know it can be?"

I had to tell him that there is no novel.

"Do I ever finish the book?"

"If you finished it, it has been lost. Maybe in your effort to get to America, and struggling to build your farm and provide for your family, you never took the time or found the time to return to finish the story. It never became a classic, because you never published it." I felt his disappointment, his sense of self-betrayal, his displeasure with the circumstances of life that kept him from his calling.

Giovanni challenged me. "What about you? You going to let your mother's story die with her?"

I told Giovanni about my dream that night in 1990 when I had slept in the mountains just off the peak of San Bernardo Grande. I continued, "I had a dream lush with golden wheat fields producing perpetual grain, corn stalks spawning multiple ears, chickens laying eggs every half-hour, and a woman bearing child after child after child after child. In my dream it all seemed perfectly normal. Startled out of the dream at four a.m., I realized the woman who was at home amongst this prolific vista was my mother and your granddaughter. Her life was a salient affirmation of humanity, and there was a story here that had to be told.

"I could not go back to sleep because the urge to tell this story was too strong, and I finished the first three chapters before the sun rose, and an additional fifty-three chapters in the next two months. In this episodic work I named *The Book of Agnes,* we see the heroine raising a garden, butchering, hosting the thrashers, worshipping, participating in the annual church picnic, suffering from temptation, raising her children, gently pushing them toward a religious life, surviving a disastrous fire, inheriting your farm, losing her husband, losing her mind, and eventually coming to terms with her calling as mother, finding the self she never sought to know."

Almost as an afterthought, I added, "If I was to give a word to my mother it would be 'fertile.' If I had to describe, in only one word, America between World War I and the Vietnam War—after you died, we lived in a world defined by its wars—it would be 'fertile.' If I was to give a word to Wisconsin, or to Genoa—that's the new name for Bad Ax— it would be 'fertile.' Agnes was both a product and a maker of those prolific times and places."

Giovanni's voice: "Did it become a best seller? Can I read a copy? Is it the *Aeneid* of America?"

I had to tell him no. The book was episodic, but hardly the Great American Epic; it never sold even one copy, for the draft lay buried in my computer waiting to be rediscovered and completed. I explained, "I never had time to finish the book; I became too busy." I explained how demanding it had been to make international clown-theater and mime festivals. That I started a second family, renovated some houses, mowed too many lawns, enjoyed too many carnivals, meandered too many times to the ice-cream parlor, started teaching again, wrote other books that seemed more important at the time.

"Bull cocky. Excuses, all of them. Write it."

I responded as much to myself as to Giovanni. "I want to find here in 'Venerville' the muse to help me return to this story, which I know needs desperately to be told, and I know I am the one who has to tell it. Like you, I am confident this story will be of wide interest." I turned to Giovanni. "Come on, tell me your story. Tell me Margherita's story. She could be the muse to provide me with the truth I need, to turn my loose episodes about your granddaughter into a story of epic height." He just looked at me. "I'll tell you what. If you tell me Margherita's story, I'll write it. I'll let the world know what you failed to tell them." He did. I will. At the moment her story is still waiting for the words necessary to give it justice. Still, I know I can and will write her story.

Giovanni looked west; I turned my head to see the last sliver of the almost-full moon slip from sight, looking as if the mountain swallowed it. I turned back, but Giovanni had slipped away. I turned north and slowly walked into the town, hoping to be engulfed, now wanting to meet Margherita as well as find Giovanni again. I took picture after picture of the individual houses. None of them spoke out, "This is great-grandpa's house." Still, it seemed certain that Giovanni and Margherita and her husband Primo had visited every one of these houses: to court, visit a relative, care for an ill relative, share a Sunday dinner, play checkers, attend a wake, or just gossip.

I stopped at the Immaculate Conception Church (where I assumed the Veners had worshipped), which stood modestly on the west side of Via Prestone, the name of S.S. 36 for the length of this borough. I decided to step in. But when I opened the gate and took the two steps to the door, I found it locked. Who were they locking out or in? Certainly, they did not think they could lock in Mary or Jesus, and it was a stretch of the imagination to think anyone in "Venerville" would abscond with even a pamphlet, let alone a sanctified object. I don't believe the doors of Saint Charles Church in Genoa, Wisconsin, were ever locked. After all, someone might want to pray at three a.m. I'd known my mother to hike over to Saint Charles at five a.m. to pray for my soul when she couldn't sleep. I had no reason to think her great-grandmother Margherita Della Morte-Venner had not done the same thing for Giovanni's soul, especially after he had run off to that wild, godforsaken place called America. In the 1850s the church probably did not have locks. It was obvious that the out-of-place, ominous, iron mechanism that was bolted into the door and held tight with a massive hinge lock had been added long after the church had begun serving this community. Still, the lock was old and rusty, and it was clear they had been locking people out for a long, long time. I wondered if they locked the doors in Genoa now. I concluded they must. Certainly, the world has changed since I struck out on my own from Genoa in 1956 at the ripe old age of fourteen. But I did not see that change here, in Vho or San Bernardo, and for that matter, I didn't see it later when I returned to Genoa. I think neither has a reason to fear vandalism, and by unlocking their doors it might say we can trust each other once again. But I am a hopeless romantic about the possibilities of humans being good if you just take the time to expect positive behavior. In my humble view, removing the locking mechanism of every door leading into every worship center in the world would send a powerful message, and the consequences might surprise the cynics.

I walked around to the back of the church, hoping to find a door that might be open. But the walkway stopped as the building came flush up against the mountainside. I put my hands on the wall of the church, hoping that Primo and Margherita might notice I was there and say hello, but nothing happened. I picked up a rock to carry a reminder of this moment back to America and walked back to the front. Giovanni leaned against the old fence, peering at what might once have been the burial ground of a former pastor or a rich patron, maybe even a Vener, but was now a tiny yard where parishioners could gather. I crossed over to walk up the other side of the church. This time the path was blocked by a fence. I leaned against the fence so I could fix my eyes on the church in an effort to burn its image and meaning onto my memory. The church was small, unimpressive, the kind of worship space I usually find uplifting. But it was cold, neither reminding me that I was something bigger (like the Hermanson chapel at Davis and Elkins College in Elkins, West Virginia) or that I was an insignificant speck of dust (as does Bishop Treacy's tomblike cathedral in La Crosse, Wisconsin). Nor did it embrace me as a member of a community, like Saint Charles Church in Genoa, Wisconsin, could. No, it seemed to say that life is pretty dull; put up with it, and show up here on Sunday so I can remind you. The sign on the door said there were services at 9:00 a.m. and at 11:30 a.m. The sign was old, so I wasn't sure if I could come back to be transformed by what I presumed was its internal beauty, suggesting, "OK, life looks pretty dull here, but you can have a beautiful and rich soul and mind." But I couldn't come back anyway, for I would be on my way to San Bernardo by nine a.m., and I had no intention of returning by eleven thirty. They had locked me out, and it hurt. Later, I learned this church was not built until some years after Giovanni had left Campodolcino for Genoa.

I stood a while longer in the tiny yard that might once have held my ancestors' remains, then edged my way back to the gate and continued my walk up the street alone. The silence was broken for a moment as a car roared through the street as if it were on a superhighway. I wondered where its driver had to go in such a hurry on a sleepy Sunday morning. I concluded he had nowhere to go; he just had to prove to himself he was man enough to push the pedal to the metal.

I came upon a little side road that reminded me of the turn onto Venner Hollow Road in Genoa, where Giovanni had staked his claim, changed his name to John, married Bart Sterlocchi's sixteen-year-old daughter, and fathered ten children, including my grandfather Bartholomew "Tom" Venner. Suddenly Giovanni was back. I asked him if he lived up this road, if there was something here that prompted him to choose those three forty-acre plots just outside Bad Ax City where my brother, William Pedretti, still lives. Like this street in Prestone, it was not hidden, but you could drive by it fifty times and not notice it. It was right there by the main road, yet a house located in this alley would feel out of the way, psychologically isolated from the rest of the community. Silence. I was now seriously searching for the house where Giovanni and his father and grandfather had been born. Before me was a tall, green, stucco, five-story house that looked nothing like the house Giovanni had built for his family just off Route 56 a mile or so from Bad Ax City on a dead-end trail now called Venner Hollow Road. Still, the house beckoned me to pay attention, and I felt an urge to enter. Of course, I couldn't knock on the door of a perfect stranger at six o'clock in the morning. Plus, what would I say? I knew only a few Italian words, and chances are the owners spoke no English. Giovanni showed no sign of recognition. I have no reason to trust my instincts about things like this, and yet for me that was the house where Giovanni grew up and where he said goodbye to his parents as he headed toward the land of possibilities called Bad Ax City, where his friends and relatives had settled just a year or two before. "Hey, Giovanni, is this where you were raised? It feels like I've been here." More silence.

I continued along that side road and walked by more houses, each feeling farther and farther from the hubbub of downtown Prestone, but none were more than a couple of minutes' walk from the center. The road arched back just below where I had parked the car. My imaginary great-grandfather and I shuffled our way back up the street, both of us pensive and engaged at the same time. I continued north along the Splugen Road to the northern edge of Prestone. Along the way I picked up two pebbles that looked like they had been kicked out of the way some 150 years ago by a young man dreaming of getting the hell out of a place where even the church said life is plain and meant to be dull; let's avoid conflict and challenge; let's neither advance nor retreat, just hold. But he did not want to "hold," so he kicked that little rock out of his way and thought, "I don't need to walk on this pebble forever, I can kick it out of my way and head west." Yes, this is what I was thinking; who knows what Giovanni thought? I put the stones in my pocket and now both sit on my night stand, a symbol of how easy and how hard it is to stay put, and how hard and mysterious it is to get up and move halfway around the world in a ship relying on wind power, to a place overrun with centuries of trees.

As I walked out of the village proper, Lake Prestone stood boldly in front of me. A Prestonian and his son were tossing fishing lines into the lake in hopes of catching an early fish or, more likely, just to be with each other in the quiet of this morning. They stood watching the floats on their lines bopping in the water, while I stood watching them watching. This could have been Giovanni and Primo. I've never met a Venner who was not up before the crack of dawn, and I had no reason to doubt that, had I come here in 1850, I would have found them leaning over the lake from a protruding rock, eagerly awaiting the first catch of the day. I snapped a picture of this moment, even though I will never forget this tableau, etched so perfectly before the morning mountain, jutting up behind Portarezza, the commune just across the lake. I continued walking along the lake and came upon a solo fisherman who was guiding a fish that had dared to take his bait along the lakeshore, so he could plop it onto a wet rock. It was a small fish, but bigger than many my father used to bring home after a few hours on the Mississippi River. The angler took out a glove so he wouldn't touch the fish with his own flesh, and he carefully released its mouth from the hook. I thought, "What a sissy, he won't even touch the fish."

Tenderly and with clear respect, he tossed the fish back into the lake. A good man whom I had instantaneously misjudged. By now I was standing on the north bridge, and the water was rushing underneath me as if it were desperate to get into Lake Prestone where it could chill out. Boy, did I ever identify with that feeling. Working in the theater and producing international festivals, I had countless times encountered the mad rush that brought hundreds, sometimes thousands, of details to complete and mesh together at the last hour before opening night—and the great relief the next day when madness merged into achievement. From where I stood, I had a complete view of the town. I stopped and let that view burn onto my memory cells. All my life I had preferred lakes to oceans, mountains and hills to open fields, quiet to hubbub. That's what was before me; a lake stretching across a serene valley that united with the rising mountains, interrupted only by a modest dam and rows of houses that had stood so long they had become the patina of the valley.

I slapped my face; it was time to end this reverie as I was to meet Annie for breakfast at seven thirty, and I was also expecting a call from Valentina Via to confirm we would meet at eight thirty in Chiavenna, from where we would return up the mountain to San Bernardo. Here I was, in "Venerville," overlooking the town where my mother's family came from, but I was more excited to get back to San Bernardo. I had come here to get inspired to finish that book about the fertile women for which my mother served as the prototype, and I was now eager to leave "Venerville" and get to San Bernardo where my father's family was from. I loved and admired my mother, her generous spirit, her empathic soul, and her insightful, if uneducated, mind. My father, on the other hand, was mean-spirited, narrow in vision, and totally practical. Yet I was more pulled to the land of the Pedrettis. Was it because tradition made Pedretti my surname? I preferred to think that it was because the man I most admired as a child was my grandfather Peter Pedretti. On the other hand, I barely remembered my grandparents Tom and Mary Venner, who died when I was just three and four years old respectively. Even more important to my attachment to San Bernardo, perhaps, was the simple fact that I had spent my first six years on a farm that probably appealed to the original Pedretti owner, being on top of one of the highest ridges in Genoa Township, making it physically the closest thing in Genoa to living on Mount Saint Bernard.

I stopped across the street from a small, deli-like store, Alimenta Libemsmittel, and watched the owner preparing for the day. I would not be rushed; today was going to be about me. Like so many others I know, my life was too controlled by other people's agendas and the demands of this event or that event. I told myself, "Not today!" I would not be rushed out of town, and I would not let other people's schedules control mine. I had come here on a spiritual journey primarily to connect to my mother's roots; I would watch this scene that Giovanni, his mother, and her mother before her had witnessed. This was their store, where they would have shopped. I watched the owner restock the merchandise, sweep the floor, and straighten goods on the shelf. Hardly the stuff for a great painting or dramatic novel, but a satisfying moment filled with implications all the same. The one appointment I wanted to keep today was with Valentina, and I was now behind schedule, so I pulled myself toward my car. Prestone was starting to come alive, with a man walking his dog, a woman heading toward the bus stop, a couple out for a stroll, and two elderly ladies dressed for church heading toward San Antonio in Portarezza, which had an earlier Mass and maybe a more dynamic preacher.

As I drove back through town heading north to Campodolcino, a mellow sadness of loss rolled down from my head to my knees. I had come as close as possible to meeting head-on with young Giovanni Vener without actually crossing the line into insanity. It was the moment I had come for; strangely, it felt as hollow as it felt full. I had not met a real person from "Venerville," I had not met a local Vener, and I had not gotten into the church or into a house, so my voyage was defined as much by my imagination as by the place. Lost in reverie, I almost drove past the now-familiar entrance to the parking lot of Saint John the Baptist church, which the Ca' de Val hotel used for its guests.

Soon it was eight forty, so I drove to the parking lot behind Giuriani Lumberyard, where I met Valentina. She wove the 12.4 kilometers up the mountain, honking the horn at the worst hairpin curves. On the way up Valentina explained that she had to be back by noon, so we would have just a little over two hours on the mountain. It seemed a terribly short time, but I was still grateful that this trip would double the amount of time I had to explore the village. Valentina told me that her husband, Fabrizio De Stefani, was from San Bernardo and that her mother and father-in-law lived in La Palua, one of four San Bernardo hamlets. She said we would stop first at her in-laws' house, as her mother-in-law, Elsa Paiarola, was an amazing source of information about San Bernardo. Elsa's mother, Erina Tomera, had taken it upon herself to preserve as much of the history of San Bernardo as she remembered by carefully passing on the information to her daughter.

I wanted Valentina to understand that fifteen years ago I knew almost nothing about my family's roots, including where the Pedrettis and Venners were from. Maybe I had family members who knew we were from this area when I was younger, but if so, I knew nothing about it. I must have looked like a kid in a candy box when I told her how thrilled I was to be able to be in San Bernardo, whose existence I had doubted only a dozen years ago.

Valentina's in-laws, Dino and Elsa De Stefani, were waiting outside their home to greet us, and they welcomed me like a long-lost relative. Elsa told me that her mother, Erina Tomera, had lived next to Teresa Cerletti, who married Guglielmo Pedretti. She was confident they were my ancestors. I thought, "Wow, her mother knew my great-great-grandparents." She said she would take me to her mother's house, as it was identical to the house where Teresa Cerletti had lived. Elsa explained that the Cerletti house was still there and we would also see it, but it no longer looked much like it had when it was owned by the Cerletti family. She added that it had been purchased as a summer home by someone from Milan, and he had completely renovated it in the 1940s. I was ready to run to these houses when they invited me in, and Elsa asked if I would like some coffee. I realized this was a great chance to get Elsa and Dino to talk. The houses were not going away, but the opportunity to hear stories must be taken when it arises. Elsa told me that there were no Pedrettis still living in San Bernardo and that she had only ever known three Pedrettis. I joked that she had now met number four. She told me their names were Giovanni, Lucia, and Maria. Giovanni was born in San Bernardo, moved to the United States, and returned to live in San Rocco, and the house he lived in on his return was now owned by relatives. Later I found out that Giovanni was born on June 20, 1892, and had died on the couch that is still in use in this house on September 26, 1963. I believe he is the last Pedretti to have lived in San Bernardo.

Elsa informed me that the Pedrettis lived in San Rocco, the uppermost hamlet of San Bernardo. I was told that San Bernardo, a community of less than three hundred people, is made up of five hamlets: San Rocco (aka Scannabecco), Martinon, La Palua, Salina, and Pescosta. Only about a ten-minute walk from Pescosta is the village of Olmo. With only two hundred or so residents in San Bernardo, you might have thought a similar commune just a short walk away would have been good pickings to find a spouse. But it appears not to have been the case. From the beginning, the people in Olmo and San Bernardo have acted as if the other doesn't exist, except as an occasional object of scorn. Consequently, you will see a lot of Cerlettis, Pedrettis, Paiarolas, Gadolas, and Falcinellas marrying each other, and you will find some of each on both Teresa Cerletti's and Guglielmo Pedretti's ancestry. Oh well; occasional crossbreeding seemed to be preferred to a little civility.

The Cerlettis lived in Salina (one of the middle hamlets), and after coffee and a handful of stories, we headed down the hill to the Erina Tomera and Teresa Cerletti houses. I fell behind, taking pictures and trying to figure out if Elsa's mother could have known my great-great-grandmother Teresa Cerletti. I didn't know when she died, but she had her last child in 1847, and I thought she was still alive in 1898. Elsa seemed to be about my age, which means her mother would have been born after 1900. I concluded that she could have known my grandmother as a very old lady. Later I discovered that Teresa Cerletti had died much earlier, so it is more likely my great-great-grandmother Teresa was the great-aunt of the Teresa Cerletti who lived in this house. That would make her my second cousin a few times removed. If this is true, it is likely that this is the house where my great-great-grandmother Teresa Cerletti also grew up. The Cerletti house had been drastically remodeled (butchered) to look like a postwar box. I immediately took more interest in the house Erina Tomera's parents once owned. It was now abandoned, and we were not going to get inside, but it was an authentic, beautiful stone schist house built to last the centuries.

Elsa told me the stable attached to her mom's house belonged to the Cerlettis. This is where Teresa Cerletti's dad wintered his beasts. Even if the owners were different Cerlettis, my Teresa and her father, Stefano, would have visited this house and helped their sibling or cousin with chores from time to time. Either way, they had walked on these stones, had entered these buildings, had sat here and dreamed. Certainly, both spent many an hour here. I crawled over the fence and made my way back to the stable. I wanted my grandma to put her arms around me and give me the hug I never got from her great-grandson. While I do not believe in an afterlife, on a few occasions I have experienced a close emotional connection to people long dead, so close I sensed they were communing with me. But for that to happen the circumstances have to be correct. I need a sense of isolation (if not actually being completely alone in the space), I must have no sense that I have to soon be somewhere else, and I cannot anticipate the moment. None of those three requirements were in place. The De Stefanis understood my need for silence and for space, but I wasn't so good at letting them go out of my mind. We were on deadline, and at least for me, being on deadline is death to a spiritual experience, and I wanted way too much for Teresa to give me a hug. Still, I was able to transform myself into her shoes. I had no trouble walking with her to carry water from the village well to the goats. I watched her shovel just enough snow out of the walkway I was standing on to get to the stable to care for her animals. I looked out over the vista that Teresa must have seen every day, and I watched it through her eyes. It was both wondrous and awesome at the same time. Wondrous, because of the vastness and the beauty. The vastness provided protection—who would traverse all that distance straight up to attack a little village that had nothing to offer for the effort? The bandits, the diseases, and the floods would stay in the valley far below. But so would everything else. Not only would it stay away, but Teresa knew that she would never get to it either, whatever "it" was. I had, from time to time, wondered how the Pedrettis and Cerlettis had lived in such an isolated place for so long. I even thought of it as a godforsaken place. At the same time, I recognized how embraced Teresa could feel with the massive beauty of these mountains gripping every moment of her life, and with the love and warmth of this mountain community where everyone was related to everyone and the goal was to get though the next winter. She would have little to compare her life to, so she would not miss what she did not know. The foes who lived in Olmo were not her type. It was easy to feel blessed compared to them. If she had traveled to San Giacomo or even Chiavenna a couple of times, she likely would have found the people too strict and unfriendly and stuck on their own self-importance. San Bernardo was heaven compared to that.

I sensed her satisfaction with being here. No thieves, no floods, no plagues, and a high likelihood that she would grow up to marry a nice San Bernardo boy and have lots of children and barely a worry in her life. Why would she want to join the unknown when the known was idyllic? Having been raised in Genoa, isolated from everything, where daily tasks defined life, I felt like I could crawl inside Teresa's head and see why she gladly followed her dad's commands, was deeply content to be here, and found her life with Guglielmo bearing fifteen children meaningful, fruitful, and holy. But I could also understand why five of her sons had to get out, had to take the risk to sail to America and Chile. The risk was enormous, but to stay here was out of the question as the population began to explode in the mid-1800s, the Prussians wanted more and more young men for their wars, and the economy shrank in the face of new transportation systems. As dangerous and frightening as it was to journey to Locarno and on to Paris and The Hague, and then board a ship toward the wild frontier of the United States with barely a lira in hand, staying put was not really an option. If every young man had stayed, the place would have been overgrazed in one generation.

In my mind's eye I watched Teresa's eldest sons Guglielmo, Stefano, and Silvestro discussing endlessly if they should go or not, and if they went, how they would get there. They'd certainly heard from some friends in the valley that a few people from there had gone over to some place called Bad Ax City, where there was abundant land and ample opportunity to raise a family comfortably. Still, Stefano and his brothers did not really know the people who had gone, and they had no way to tell if those Campodolcino folks were telling the truth. They guessed that, no matter how bad it was, the adventurers who had bolted from Campodolcino would not write back and tell their folks that they had made a mistake. William, the eldest, may have argued for them to go to California, the land of sunshine. Stefano and Lorenzo must have felt safer immigrating to Bad Ax, where they knew some people and where there was more than a good chance that it was in fact a great place to live.

I rolled my hand over the stones on the stable wall. I started to look for a loose stone. There were some on the ground that had probably fallen out of the wall, but I wanted a souvenir that I knew had been part of this building that my great-great-grandmother either lived in or visited often. My eye saw it first, there in the wall: a perfect stone, big enough to say something but not too big to slide into my pocket to take home to frame and put prominently in my office, so that I could keep some of Teresa Cerletti close to me.

It was time to move on. There were more things to see, and the precious little time I had on the mountain was ticking away. I turned and looked across the small court to where Teresa had lived. It seemed criminal to see how the man from Milan had butchered this once magnificent home. It was as if the Cerletti house had been replaced. No matter. The path that ran between her stable and her house, the one I was standing on now, was the one she walked on several times every day. I dropped to my knees, laid out flat and kissed the ground. I felt a deep connection to Maria Teresa and to Guglielmo, who most certainly wooed her on the very spot I was kissing.

It was time to go up the hill to San Rocco, where my great-grandfather Stefano and all the Pedrettis before him grew up. We walked back up the hill toward the De Stefani home. I could see San Rocco ahead of me just a block or two away but straight up, and I thought this was going to take a while and we didn't have much time left. But Valentina headed directly to her car, and we drove up the two hairpin curves to San Rocco. The first thing I saw was a very large parking lot with scores of cars. San Rocco, like the other hamlets, had no streets, so this was where you parked if you lived here or were visiting. I had not seen this many cars in one spot since arriving in Campodolcino. This was the happening place. It was true that San Bernardo would be celebrating their big event of the year in two days. In San Rocco we saw people milling about. I had not seen that in any of the other hamlets, or even in Campodolcino. It really was the happening place—maybe that was why the Pedrettis had stayed put for over four hundred years. Yes, Pedrettis had been living on San Bernardo Mountain for centuries, and now their descendants were spread out over the States, dispersed throughout Italy and some parts of South America. Since I was under the impression that there were only two Pedretti lines in the world and that the fertile Pedretti family originated in San Bernardo, I assumed the vast majority of people who shared this name descended from Guglielmo the first. But I had to also remember that there were no Pedrettis left in San Bernardo. On the other hand, with so many Lombardinis, Cerlettis, and Della Mortes still living there, certainly there were plenty of people with Pedretti ancestors who could claim San Bernardo as their home.

Only a couple of families live here year-round. Since residents no longer subsist off the land, it makes little sense to brave winters isolated on the mountain. I got the impression that the more permanent residents lived in San Rocco and wintered in Chiavenna or elsewhere, not unlike so many seniors in America who live in the Northeast or Midwest and winter in Florida. They tell you they are from Prairie du Chien or Boston; they do not say they are from Miami. I was told that several houses are owned by "outsiders," many from Milan, who use the houses for weekend retreats or summer vacation homes.

We headed directly toward the house Elsa said had been owned by the last Guglielmo Pedretti to live in San Bernardo. The De Stefanis stopped to greet a young couple heading in our direction. They looked surprised but extremely delighted to run into this couple. After a few seconds, the couple also looked delighted and the chatter became more animated. Well, luck was in the air, for this couple were the current owners of the "Pedretti" house and said they would be delighted to show me the house. We did not know if Guglielmo was a relative or not, but everyone agreed that this house had been in the Pedretti family for a long time. If my great-great-grandfather wasn't raised in this house, he certainly would have taken meals there and spent many an hour visiting or playing with the children of the Pedrettis who lived there. This time I would be able to enter the house to see what it looked like, to be enclosed in the same space where Stefano Pedretti and Guglielmo 1, 2, 3, 4, and 5 before him had dined. The current owners were Remo Gadola and Cristina Cerletti. Remo's aunt had married Guglielmo Pedretti. As a Gadola, he was probably a relative of mine; maybe fourth cousin. Teresa's mother and father were both Cerlettis. As I was related to both Cerletti families that had lived in San Bernardo, it was extremely likely that Cristina and I were third or fourth cousins. But the best was still to come. Remo and Teresa had nearly finished restoring the house to its original condition. When I told them that my great-grandfather had emigrated in the early 1850s, they said the house now looked very much like it had then. They had scraped off multiple layers of paint and torn out various upgrades to restore the house to what it looked like in the mid-nineteenth century. Not only was the wood of the floor, walls, and ceilings original, some of the furniture dated back past 1850. Indoors, I saw the beauty of the wood, the clarity of the design, and the utilitarian use of space. The warm, glowing walls, ceilings, and floors would have aided the thick stone walls in their duty to make the severe winters on the mountain a little more bearable.

Cristina Cerletti gave me a thorough tour of the house. The kitchen, almost certainly the social hub of the house in earlier days, was relatively large. It reminded me of the kitchen I lived in the first six years of my life. There were some modern upgrades, such as a gas stove and a stainless-steel sink, but I had no difficulty imaging a wood stove and porcelain country sink in their place as that is what we had in our kitchen back in Genoa in 1948. The old wooden trunk reminded me where we had kept wood for the stove, and the old-fashioned table and chairs, while smaller than the table I grew up with thirteen kids around it, looked particularly familiar. In a second-floor bedroom was a rocking chair that dated back before the last Guglielmo Pedretti and most likely was in this house when my great-grandpa Stefano lived or visited here. I sat in the chair and had Valentina take my picture—I apologize, but I cannot find the words to express how elated I felt at that moment.

Across the hall was a small room now used as a guest room where the owners had once hung sausage and bresaola (dried beef) to cure. The room reminded me of the small spare room in our house on Mound Ridge where Dad and Mom would hang hundreds of pounds of sausage and dried beef. My ancestors cured their meat this way because it was the only way to preserve the fall slaughter. For my dad and mom, it was about making food that had long been a favorite of every Pedretti and Venner. Bresaola is not just ordinary dried beef. It is prepared by taking the very best cut of beef, usually the prime rib, and soaking it in brine for twenty-eight to forty days. Then it is air dried until it is cured. In this state it can hang in a cool room for months. It is several times softer than American dried beef and ten times tastier. Some people believe that bresaola was invented in the San Giacomo valley. Personally, I'd bet on it being made for the first time on the San Bernardo Mountains. For sure it had its origins in Valchiavenna, a large valley that includes all of Valle San Giacomo. To this day, the best bresaola comes from this region, and while in Lombardy I ate a few pounds of it that was as tasty as what my mother and father made. As a kid, we had dried sausage that compares to nothing else I have ever eaten. To this day I rarely eat sausage, as it always tastes like an inferior brand. When in Campodolcino I purchased a stick from the Alimentari store, and it was nearly as good as the sausage my dad made. It is reported that there are members of the Genoa, Wisconsin, community that still make a sausage that tastes the same as that once made on the mountains of San Rocco.

On the way down the stair-ladder, we stopped to enter the root cellar. The original owners had installed a root cellar to preserve their harvests, and the current owners kept fresh pickings from their garden, bottles of wine, grappa, and soft drinks chilled inside the stone walls carved into the mountainside. After the informative tour, we settled down at the kitchen table. I thought, *There is every likelihood I am sitting at the very same table on the very same chair that Stefano and his father and even grandfather had used.* In the search for a connection to the past, is it possible to get better?

Cristina asked if I would like an espresso, and Remo bought out a bottle of homemade grappa to flavor the coffee. Not only had Remo and Cristina made the grappa, they had picked the Iva herb used to make the grappa from the surrounding mountain. That's what they had been doing earlier in the day, and when we saw them in the alley they were on their way back from an unsuccessful hunt to find more Iva. I was told of an old saying: "Herb Iva makes a dead man alive." Some say the brew cleans out your intestines; others say it's so strong it jolts you back to life. As Remo poured the grappa into my cup, I could not help but notice that the bottle he was using once held Vener Grappa. No longer manufactured, Vener Grappa was of high repute in its day and was the last grappa commercially made in the Val San Giacomo.

It was time to get back. Already Valentina had called her husband twice to extend our stay, and she had also called Luigi on my behalf to tell him we were running late. Reluctantly we said our goodbyes. I thought that the one thing that could top this experience would be to get into the San Rocco Chapel. I had not even asked to do so; I had been told that it was privately owned and had been closed for some time. The church had been built following the Great Plague of Milan (1629-1631), which had devastated the area from Switzerland to Milan and beyond. The people of San Bernardo prayed to San Rocco, the patron saint of good health, and promised him they would build a chapel in his honor if he protected them from the plague. I was informed that not one San Bernardo resident caught the plague, and the community banded together to build the church. I told Elsa I was disappointed I could not get in the church, as it would have been the place of worship for the Pedretti family for the two hundred years from its construction until Stefano Pedretti immigrated to Genoa. Besides, it was late, and we had to leave. But Elsa saw a man in his backyard who she suspected had the key to the church. She yelled down to him that I was there and would like to get into the church. He went immediately into his house to get the key and had opened the church by the time we walked down the hill. While it had few direct similarities to Saint Charles Church in Genoa, Wisconsin, it did have the feel that Saint Charles had when I was a boy. These were places of neither aspiration nor oppression. Eugene Raskin in his book *Architecturally Speaking* wrote that churches were designed either to send the message that you were extremely important in the eyes of God because you were part of humanity that was capable of creating such an inspiring space, or to send the message that you were an unimportant zero in the face of a wondrous God and massive architecture. San Rocco and Genoa's Saint Charles churches did neither. These spaces were not designed to inspire or depress but to encourage a coming together with fellow humans, with nature, with the universe. San Rocco had that small, intimate feel that I remembered Saint Charles once had, and it made you want to kneel and pray. They both said, "Here is a place where you can rethink your life." I had not voluntarily knelt in a church in over forty years, but I found myself kneeling before the altar of San Rocco Church—not to pray to a God I no longer believed in, but to worship all the same.

Now it really was time to get back, so we dropped Elsa and Dino off at their house and said a quick goodbye. Traveling down the mountain, I rambled on to Valentina about how precious this time was and how dear she was to have made it possible for me to experience San Bernardo on this level.

Nancy and Annie were waiting for me at our hotel with the suitcases ready to toss in the car and a sandwich for me to eat as we drove the three blocks to Luigi Fanetti's house. Hunger was so far from my mind that I could only nibble on the sandwich. We arrived at Luigi and Pina's house about two fifteen p.m., more than ninety minutes later than the original plan. They invited us in and introduced us to the rest of their family. Luigi gave me an updated copy of the siblings of my great-grandfather Stefano Pedretti and a copy of my ancestral chart that he had prepared with six generations, including a couple of names and dates I did not already have. I asked if he had more generations, and he proceeded to print out seventy-two additional ancestors of my great-grandparents Madeline Sterlocchi, Stefano Pedretti, and John Venner, all who had immigrated to America in the 1850s. This gave me a total of nine generations. When I later had the opportunity to study the charts, I discovered that Luigi and his cohort Dino Buzzetti had added sixty-seven new ancestors to our family tree. To the best of my knowledge, no one in America had this information.

I learned, with Alberto Cerletti's help, they had discovered that my great-grandfather Stefano had four more siblings than we previously had records about. Susanne Pedretti had gotten information on Stefano and ten of his siblings when she visited San Bernardo in 1996. The new research showed there were four additional siblings listed in a different record book in the San Bernardo Church. It appears that one document listed the eleven siblings who were deceased by the time of the writing, and the other document listed the four who were known or presumed to be alive at the time.

The oldest son of the last Pedretti ancestor to live his entire life in San Bernardo was, as we should have suspected, not my great-grandfather Stefano, but Guglielmo, named after his Grandfather Guglielmo Pedretti. We knew that Guglielmo, Stefano's brother, had come to America with him along with Stefano's younger brother Sylvester. And we knew that the brothers were reportedly twenty-eight, twenty-seven, and twenty-six years old. But the information collected in 1996 showed that Stefano's brother Guglielmo was born nine years after Stefano. That did not agree with the reported ages, but it was what we had. We also knew that this Guglielmo immigrated to California and left his brothers in Genoa. That seemed odd, as he would have been only eighteen years old. But people were bolder in those days and, as I said, it was the only data we had.

On further inspection it was noticed that the document in San Bernardo indicated that the Guglielmo Pedretti who was born nine years after Stefano had died the same day he was born. Apparently it was overlooked that the document stated that the rest of the family could be found in a different record book in Tablet 16. There, the page listed the oldest son, Guglielmo (born on April 8, 1825), and noted that he had moved to the United States. Also listed were three younger sisters. On two other pages that I received after returning to the United States, the documents noted that Guglielmo was living in Chile. Some of my cousins had earlier made an unsuccessful effort to find out what had happened to Guglielmo after my grandfather last saw him around 1890, and if he had any living offspring. This new data led to records kept in a church in Chile indicating that Guglielmo had married in 1869.

Then I went over the books and land plots that I had given to Luigi on the first day, to make sure he understood what was there. I pointed out on the map where some of the people he had researched owned farms. I got the impression that Luigi thought most of the immigrants had settled in the village of Genoa. In fact, with few exceptions, they became farmers when they arrived along the Mississippi River shore in the far western part of Wisconsin. I also went over some of the pictures I had given him, explaining who was in them and how they related to his research.

Soon it was three o'clock and time to say goodbye. We took some last-minute photos, climbed into our car, and slowly drove out of Campodolcino. As we left, I had Nancy take a picture of the sign at the south end of town that said "You are leaving Campodolcino." Actually, the sign had the name Campodolcino with a line through it—the universal meaning of "no," as in "no entrance" or "no exit." So it literally said "No more Campodolcino." I was not ready to accept that; I knew I had to come back, and I will.

9 August 2009 – Sunday morning
Prestone, Campodolcino, Sondrio, Lombardy, Italy

The waning moon before it set behind Pizzo Truzzo, the mountain just west of Campodolcino where the Pedrettis once grazed their livestock in the summer

Prestone, home of Giovanni Vener
and many of his ancestors

Looking down a quiet street on an early Sunday
morning. 9 August 2009

Giovanni Battista Vener
John Venner
Giovanni was the first Vener to immigrate to Genoa.
Shortly after arriving in the United States he changed his
name to John Venner. His story is told in Book VII.
Only known photograph
Circa 1880

Owner of Alimenta Libemsmittel
seen preparing for the day.
Prestone
Early Sunday morning, 9 August 2009

**Fishing on Sunday morning in Prestone,
Campodolcino**
9 August, 2009

Dino and Elsa De Stefani and their daughter Valentina Via

posing for photo as they took a break in telling the San Bernardo story.

Historic documents

opened to pages where we found Pedretti ancestral trails used to build our family tree.

2009

Former Home of Guglielmo & Maria Teresa Pedretti

These are photographs of what is left of the home where Stefano Pedretti and his 14 siblings were born and raised. The house burned down in 1999 when a gust of wind blew embers from the fireplace while the owner was away. The house is waiting to be reconstructed.

This view of Guglielmo Maria and Maria Teresa Pedretti's house is what they would have seen as they walked home from the village or the fields. The top of the main entrance door can be seen just left of the boy walking toward the camera.

Below - Cerletti Home

Elsa De Stefani standing in front of a house believed to have been identical and next door to the home of Maria Teresa Cerletti. The Cerletti house was "modernized" in the 1950s and no longer looks like this.

View from Pedretti home in Salina

Looking down at the San Bernardo Church, you can see how close Olmo, the town in the background, is. Because of the rivalry between the two towns, each community had their own parish and pastor and there are very few recordings of marriages between families of the two towns.

Former Home of Giovanni Pedretti (1892-1963)

Photograph of the author inside the home of Giovanni Pedretti the last Pedretti to make San Rocco, San Bernardo his home. The current owners have restored the home to what they believe is its original state. Stefano Pedretti would have visited this home often as close relatives lived here when he grew up in San Bernardo.

Current owners of G. Pedretti House

Dino De Stefani, Remo Gadola, Elsa De Stefani, Valentina Via and Cristina Cerletti at entrance of Pedretti house. Remo Gadola and Christina Cerletti had recently restored the home to its original condition. Both are distance relatives of the author.

San Rocco Chapel
Borgo di San Bernardo frazione di San Giacomo
Filippo

Two views from Starleggia
Starleggia was the original home of the Starlochi
family. Majestic mountains are visible in all directions. The
town in the valley in bottom photograph is Campodolcino.

Arrivederci

"Soon it was three o'clock and time to say good-bye. We took some last minute photos, got into our car and slowly drove out of Campodolcino."

From left to right: Luigi Fanetti, Michael Pedretti, Felice Gelfi, Giuseppina "Pina" Fanetti , Maddalena Pilatti, Fabio Hylton, Chiara Pilatti, Michela Fanetti, and Claudia Fanetti with Bella.

Photo by Nancy Hill

SIGN AS YOU LEAVE CAMPODOLCINO
No more Campodolcino,
A tourist locality
1,071 m (3,514 ft.) above sea level
"See you soon"

Postscript

I wanted to make our last stop the Santuario di Madonna in Gallivaggio. When we had stopped at this church on the way into town, I knew two things about it. Most importantly, I knew that my great-great-grandparents Bartholomew Starlochi and Marianna Zaboglio had been married there about five years before they immigrated to America. I also knew that it was believed that the Virgin Mary had appeared to two young peasant girls at this spot in the fifteenth century, and that the church had been built to honor that fact. While in Valle San Giacomo, I found out that most of my ancestors from Campodolcino, Vho, Lirone, etc., would have been married in that church. They got married there because it was the most beautiful church in the valley and because they believed that the Madonna would bestow upon them extra protection from the trials of life. There could have been as many as seven generations of two separate family lines married there between 1510 and 1850. That's thirty-two couples on each side for a total of 128 people. I believe it would be reasonable to assume that about half of them got married there. That is a lot of weddings. I had to stop, see the place once more, and take in the simple fact that I may have had as many as one hundred ancestors exchange vows while standing on the exact same floor that I would soon stand on.

Before we got to San Giacomo, we crossed the river Liro to get a better perspective of Prestone. As we proceeded toward the Santuario di Madonna, Nancy took pictures of the "Welcome to Lirone" and "Compaginare" signs. I had learned that some of the Buzzettis had lived in these towns, and since there was not time to visit them, there was at least time to photograph the welcome signs to remind me to visit and look more deeply into these villages at a later time.

I was keen on getting some pictures of Santuario di Madonna and touching the rock. But there were several people praying, and it seemed terribly out of place to do either, so I embraced the space and imagined grandparent after grandparent walking down the aisle to wed. Ultimately, all those marriage vows led to an enormous amount of people spread all over the world, including the one standing in this church, who now lived a stone's throw from Sesame Place in New Falls Township, a suburb of Philadelphia, Pennsylvania.

Genoa, Wisconsin: From Bad Ax to Genoa

Photograph taken circa 1910

Genoa, Wisconsin

For *The Story of Our Stories*, Genoa, Wisconsin, holds center stage. The coulees, bluffs, riverbed, and maybe even the pigeons called out to our immigrants to make it home; it cuddled the second generation, shaped the third, and will forever define who future generations are to become.

Genoa Village is a community in Vernon County, Wisconsin, at latitude 433436N and longitude 0911327W.

Genoa Township is located 72 through 84 miles directly north of the Wisconsin-Illinois Border and 0 to 24 miles east of the Mississippi River. If the boundary line between Iowa and Minnesota were extended across the Mississippi, it would strike about the center of section 21 of the town (in the southwest corner). Genoa is located in Wisconsin Townships 12 and 13 north. Specifically, it is comprised of Township 12, range 6 west, Sections 5–8 and 17–20; Township 12 north, range 7 west, sections 1–4, 10–16, and 21–24; and Township 13 north, range 7 west, sections 21–28 and 33–36. The total land area of approximately 22,500 acres is less than a full township of 23,040 acres.

# # #

Hastings Landing to Bad Ax City to Genoa

They did not come for the streets paved in gold but for the fields of dirt—black dirt never before disturbed by human hand or till. Decomposing plant life, chaste air, and uncorrupted rain had mingled for millennia and now seemed to open its hand for their seeds of clover, corn, and oats. Forests standing guard over the cliffs appeared ready for the ax. They came up the Mississippi river to Hastings Landing (later renamed Genoa), having abandoned the lead mines of death in Galena, Illinois.

For the century of primary interest to our story, 1854–1954, life in Genoa, Wisconsin centered on the farm. Farmers bred and raised pigs, chickens, and cows. Everyone had a large garden and ate fresh vegetables and fruits in season and canned ones when not in season. Milk came from their own cows and eggs from the chickens. Most butchered a cow or two, a deer, and a couple of pigs every fall. Squirrel was a staple in the fall. Fresh fish was fried to perfection when the farmer had time to fish. The remaining meat came from chickens that were beheaded as needed. Some things were purchased at the store: flour, sugar, and spices were used for baking bread, cakes, and pies. Cornflakes and Quaker Oats made an easy and inexpensive breakfast. For a special treat, households might buy a dozen hot dogs or a gallon of ice cream. Most farmers had three outfits: one to wear, one for the wash, and one for Sunday dress-up. If you were the second son or daughter, you might never wear a brand-new piece of clothing until your wedding day. For the adult women, Easter could be an excuse to get a new hat or, in a good year, a whole new outfit.

Before Genoa was a farm community it was a river town, and its name was Bad Ax. Settlement in the coulee just north of Bad Ax River followed the building of a landing used to refuel steamships. The first settlers were rough, tough, hard-drinking lumberjacks, and the name Bad Ax City seemed more than appropriate. In 1853, some settlers from Campodolcino, Italy, joined some settlers from Airolo, Switzerland, to head upriver from Galena, Illinois, in hopes of establishing a settlement where they could take up farming and trade. In Galena they worked the lead mines, a common means of livelihood for new immigrants. Some had worked the lead mines back home; at some point they may have asked, "Why'd we cross the ocean if we are going to do what we did back home for less pay and more hours?"

They sent Giuseppe Monti, born in Airolo, north to search for some virgin land where they could plant crops and raise cows and hogs with instructions to stay close to the river so they could easily ship the fruits of their labor to markets. When his boat stopped off at the fuel stop for steamships navigating the river just north of Bad Ax River, Monti spotted their paradise. The land was ready for the taking; there was already an established landing for boats, and lumberjacking could provide income until they made their farms and trade operations profitable. According to Ernesto R. Milani in a paper he presented in Annapolis, Maryland, on November 4, 2004, for the thirty-seventh conference of the American Italian Historical Association, Monti thought this area—a few miles north of the Bad Ax

River massacre—"was suitable for many reasons: wild pigeons, rolling hills that resembled the Alpine panorama of the migrants and a route that led up north toward the lumber camps of Wisconsin and Minnesota" (p. 6). Monti grabbed the next steamboat going downriver and soon returned with six families who had emigrated from Campodolcino and Airolo. They sent word back home about their new life and encouraged family and friends to join them in this land rich in trees, river life, and soil. Within a year many from both areas traveled to La Havre in France to catch a ship across the Atlantic to New York, from the New York Central Railway to Chicago, and then west on foot or by horse and carriage to the bluffs and coulees just north of where the Bad Ax River flowed into the Mississippi.

Monti received a patent for the area along the Mississippi River north of section 9 and south of section 17 and by 1854 had laid out a plat for Bad Ax City. One of the first immigrants to purchase one of the 162 plats was Joseph Morelli, who built a replica of a San Giacomo stone house at the foot of what would become known as the Genoa Bluff. The house was set high enough to avoid damage from the raging Mississippi River and low enough to be easily accessible to and from the river. The house, built by an Italian stone smith, was still occupied a century later. Other early customers included the Pedretti brothers from San Bernardo, who threw up a temporary barn-house in late 1854 that remained their home for fourteen years.

In just two years, the town had a hotel, a post office, a school building, a shop that manufactured wagons, a visiting preacher, a wedding, a funeral, and the birth of a child by an immigrant. Most astonishing, they had a full-time physician—Dr. Bugaizy, an Italian, who emigrated from Galena, Illinois. "He secured a good practice among his people and remained for about four years," according to an 1884 work called *History of Vernon County, Wisconsin* (p.   272, https://archive.org/stream/historyofvernonc01spri/historyo fvernonc01spri_djvu.txt).

Many of the first settlers to the new town came from the Val San Giacomo (Valley of Saint James the Lesser) in Northern Italy and from nearby Airolo, Switzerland. All were Italian, and many knew each other back in the old country. They had no illusions of getting rich quick but sought instead a place to establish roots, raise their children, and rest in peace. Only a handful came with enough money to make the down payment on a forty-acre plat or two. The United States government had divided the territory into townships composed of thirty-six sections, with each section being one square mile. Each section was divided into quarter sections, which were further subdivided into four plats of forty acres each. These forties were available for fifty-two dollars and could be had for a down payment of twelve cents an acre, with ten years to pay off the balance. If you had a team of horses and a plow, you might get hired by an absentee owner to plow his acres for up to three dollars each.[2] You could earn that down payment in a week. The problem was, no one could afford to buy a plow, let alone a team of horses—not to mention finding an absentee landlord in search of a plowman. That meant most

---

[2] "Historic Remanences," *Wisconsin Citizen*, Broadhead, WI, February 1898.

newcomers had to find work in the lumber trade or retail businesses and save pennies until they had the 480 ($4.80) needed to make a down payment on a sixteenth of a section.

They found the fields more fertile than their wildest dreams, the hillsides forested with trees to build and heat their homes, and large deposits of limestone. But they also found something else buried deep in those hills. It was invisible but every bit as real as the limestone waiting to be crushed into gravel to build their roads. True, many were so focused on planting, raising chickens and pigs, and milking cows that they failed to see it, but it shaped who they were and how they lived even more than the fields of soil and the cows of Holstein and Guernsey. There can be no question that the rich deposits of vegetation lay just beneath the surface because the prior inhabitants used these lands with deep respect and care; they may have also left behind the spiritual energy that played a role in shaping the Genoese character.

Compassion, consideration, and contentment flow through the coulees and settle on the bluffs. Whenever the ambitions of the American dream want to seep in, it has been drowned before it was recognized. The moment one thought about getting ahead off the back of his neighbor (and most never had this thought), the impulse was pricked midair and deflated before any noticed. You could make the case that consideration was so ingrained in their Saint James genes that the possibility of being sucked into the American white man's vortex of "get ahead at any cost" was not within the options of their nature. Their ancestors had avoided war for over one thousand years by avoiding ambition. Certainly this was part of the *raison d'être* for the gentle nature of the peoples who had gravitated to the bluffs and coulees that shaped Genoa Township. But the Saint James gene cannot account for the gentle nature of those who emigrated from other locales. We are all familiar with places like Sedona, known for their power and magic. Places that purport to "stimulate sensitivity permitting people to realize true dreams and ambitions," "empowerment," "a place of great power." The coulee defined by the Genoa Bluff, encompassing the village of Genoa, following Highway 56 east leading to and including Mound Ridge, is not a vortex of power but a spray drift of empathy. The Genoa Drift is so calm you think nothing can happen, for the serene microbes infiltrate every nerve with germs of satisfaction into all who stand in her vapors. I believe the Winnebago and their predecessors nurtured the Drift every bit as much as they nurtured the black earth. When married to the Saint James the Lesser genes, the Genoa Drift cross-pollinates gentleness, compassion, and empathy into kindness. This powerful force has defined who the Genoese are and makes it a safe bet that the next generation of Genoese descendants will contribute to the elimination of war and starvation.

The first generation of immigrants cleared the land to maximize their gift from nature (more accurately characterized as stolen from the Winnebago) and built cabins and barns to protect their families and their animals; the second planted seeds that feed ten times their family; the third pursued dreams; the fourth is seeking a less violent way; and the fifth and sixth possess the potential to plant the ideas that will free us from the yokes of class, race, and sex discrimination.

Latitude 433436N and longitude 0911327W identifies the village of Genoa, a place on the eastern side of the Mississippi River about eighteen miles south of La Crosse, Wisconsin, and forty-two miles north of Prairie du Chien, Wisconsin. The drive between La Crosse and Prairie du Chien is one of the most beautiful anywhere, with the forested bluffs and coulees framing the Mississippi River while also forcing it to roam a little to the left and then a little to the right as it makes its way toward the Gulf of Mexico. This area was first settled by humans around ten thousand years ago and had been occupied by various tribes until settlers from European countries displaced most natives. The Ioway, Kickapoo, Ho-Chunk, and Sauk had hunted, fished and farmed the land at different times. The Winnebago hunted here when Black Hawk moved into the territory in 1832 with high hopes that the locals would help him resist the advancing American army.

The settlers from European countries operated under a pretend system that if more than one of them settled in an area, they could claim vast portions of land for the monarchy in Europe where they had been born. That is exactly what happened in 1671 when Daumont de Saint-Lusson told a gathering of Native American leaders from what became Wisconsin that the region was now under the protection of the French government. *Voilà*, the land shared by several tribes now belonged to the Louis XIV, the King of France, because a handful of French colonizers—through their spokesman de Saint-Lusson—proclaimed it to the leaders of several thousand natives. Not 100 percent sure this was "sufficiently definitive," seven years later Nicholas Perrot, recently bankrupt, convened several tribes and negotiated a treaty giving New France dominion "not only over the territory of the upper Mississippi" but "to other places more remote." What is now Genoa, along with all of what is now Wisconsin plus more, "passed quietly into the possession of the French king." It would be another hundred years before a European, Pierre LaPoisette, set foot for the first time in 1777 in the area around Genoa. The Sauk and Winnebago who lived and hunted along the Mississippi River, unbeknownst to them, had been "French subjects" and then "British subjects" for a century by this time. The British had laid claim to the area on September 9, 1760, when the French surrendered Canada to the British. Lest there was any doubt of their domination, the British sent eighteen soldiers to occupy a post located in the Green Bay area, ostensibly to protect a handful of traders who lived there.

In 1763 the soldiers abandoned the post, but British victory over Chief Pontiac reassured the invaders that the Northwest was indeed British territory. Ten years later the United States technically "acquired" this region in the Treaty of Paris in 1783, when the British ceded the territory to the newly independent colonies as part of the treaty to end the American Revolutionary War. What would become Wisconsin had only two settlements at this time, the one in Green Bay and one in Prairie du Chien; the latter had a population of four. Despite the treaty, the British, using the excuse that some of their merchants had not been paid as agreed in the treaty, continued to occupy the Northwest Territory. Just the same, within four years Congress enacted in the Northwest Ordinance of 1787 the methodology of how to survey and subdivide the Northwest Territory

(Ohio, Indiana, Illinois, Michigan, and Wisconsin) into mile-square sections with sixteen forty-acre plots in each. In other words, this land, which was occupied by over a half dozen Native American tribes and a scattering of white settlers, was, according to British behavior and American law, the property of the king of England and the United States of America at the same time. The Jay Treaty demanded the British evacuate the area by June 1, 1796, and provided that British citizens could either leave, stay and keep their British citizenship, or stay and become American citizens. However, if they stayed and did not declare their British citizenship in one year, they would automatically become American citizens. Most settlers, largely unaware of what was happening, became American citizens by default or ignorance and with no fanfare on June 1, 1797. Similarly, the people who were Sauk, Fox, Winnebago, Menominee, Chippewa, Ottawa, Pottawattamie, and Sioux, without consent, became subject to American law.

Even while the British occupied the Northwest Territory, the American government coerced several Native American tribes to sign what is known as the Treaty of Greenville on August 3, 1795. The actual title of the agreement is: "A Treaty of Peace between the United States of America, and the Tribes of Indians called the Wyandots, Delawares, Shawnees, Ottawas, Chippewas, Pattawatimas, Miamis, Eel Rivers, Weas, Kickapoos, Piankeshaws, and Kaskaskias." The treaty stated:

> Article 1: Henceforth all hostilities shall cease; peace is hereby established, and shall be perpetual.

> Article 3 [paraphrased]: The American Indians agreed to relinquish all claims to land south and east

of a boundary that began roughly at the mouth of the Cuyahoga River. The Indians, however, could still hunt on the land that they ceded.

Article 4: The United States relinquish their claims to all other Indian lands northward of the river Ohio, eastward of the Mississippi, and westward and southward of the Great Lakes and the waters, uniting them, according to the boundary line agreed on by the United States and the King of Great Britain, in the treaty of peace made between them in the year 1783. [Note: this included all of what would become Wisconsin.]

Article 5: To prevent any misunderstanding about the Indian lands relinquished by the United States in the fourth article, it is now explicitly declared, that the meaning of that relinquishment is this: the Indian tribes who have a right to those lands, are quietly to enjoy them, hunting, planting, and dwelling thereon, so long as they please, without any molestation from the United States; but when those tribes, or any of them, shall be disposed to sell their lands, or any part of them, they are to be sold only to the United States; and until such sale, the United States will protect all the said Indian tribes in the quiet enjoyment of their lands against all citizens of the United States, and against all other white persons who intrude upon the same. And the said Indian tribes again acknowledge themselves to be under the protection of the said United States, and no other power whatever.

Article 6: If any citizen of the United States, or any other white person or persons, shall presume to settle upon the lands now relinquished by the United States, such citizen or other person shall be out of the protection of the United States; and the Indian tribe, on whose land the settlement shall be made, may drive off the settler, or punish him in such manner as they shall think fit; and because such settlements, made without the consent of the United States, will be injurious to them as well as to the Indians, the United States shall be at liberty to break them up, and remove and punish the settlers as they shall think proper, and so effect that protection of the Indian lands herein before stipulated.

Even though no tribe occupying what would become Wisconsin was party to the treaty, the treaty clearly stated that the Sauk, Fox, Winnebago, Menominee, Chippewa, Ottawa, Pottawattamie, and Sioux who lived and hunted in Wisconsin were "quietly to enjoy" the land where they lived "so long as they please, without any molestation from the United States," and that "the United States will protect all the said Indian tribes in the quiet enjoyment of their lands against all . . . white persons." Furthermore, if any US citizen or noncitizen dared to settle on Native American land, then "the Indian tribe . . . may drive off the settler, or punish him in such manner as they shall think fit."

The ink on the treaty had hardly dried when white settlers "presumed to settle upon the lands now relinquished by the United States" and the government set up quarters to protect the settlers to make sure the Indian tribes dared not execute their right to "drive off the settler, or punish him in such manner as they shall think fit" for fear of massive retaliation. Still, thanks to the reserve of the natives, this treaty was followed by more than sixteen years of peace that ended only when Governor William Henry Harrison of the Indiana Territory marched a thousand soldiers into the headquarters of a confederacy of American Indians made up of various tribes that finally outwardly opposed US expansion into territory guaranteed to them in Article 4 of the Treaty of Greenville. Two brothers, Tecumseh and the Prophet, became spokespersons and leaders of the tribes who felt that the agreement Harrison had made in Fort Wayne with other tribal leaders was not in the spirit or the law of the previous treaty. Harrison wanted to expand the area where whites could settle—and he manipulated, against President James Madison's dictate, the Pottawatomie, Lenape, Eel Rivers, and Miami to come to a meeting in Fort Wayne. In the negotiations, Harrison promised large subsidies and payments to the tribes if they would cede the lands he wanted. At first the Miami refused to sign, but eventually they conceded. Others who opposed the treaty joined forces under Tecumseh and the Prophet to unite many tribes into an organized defense against the growing number of white settlers. Through this union they would defend the lands they had lived on for thousands of years and had been guaranteed the right to occupy by the US government. To stop them, Harrison marched his troops to the edge of their headquarters, and war broke out on November 7, 1811. Tecumseh was traveling, and the Prophet misled his warriors, causing them to retreat in confusion and giving the appearance of victory to Harrison.

The Battle of Tippecanoe was a precursor and a direct cause of the War of 1812, as the British had supported Tecumseh. On December 24, 1814, the Treaty of Ghent ended the War of 1812 and removed British influence from the Northwest Territory. For the first time, the United States had undisputed control of what would be later known as Vernon County, including Genoa; that is undisputed among the British, French, and Americans. The Winnebago and Sauk who lived and hunted in the area may not have agreed. Nor did the Treaty of Greenville agree; but who was concerned about the terms of agreement in a treaty that got in the way of white man's manifest destiny? There is no record of any white settlers residing in the area at the time. In fact, at the end of the war, the settlement at Green Bay, the largest in Wisconsin, was made up of about forty or fifty French Canadians.

It took only thirty more years before the Winnebago and Sauk were coerced into a treaty extinguishing forever their right to the land east of the Mississippi River, including all of Vernon County, which they had occupied for centuries. They were forced to relocate west of the Mississippi to what is now Iowa, and most of their members had been removed by 1846, the same year that Willard Spaulding built the first permanent dwelling where the village of Genoa now stands.

Even before the Treaty of Ghent, using the Jeffersonian Public Land Survey System (PLSS), the US government began to divide Wisconsin into towns and ranges composed of six-mile-square townships. Soon easterners and immigrants, especially from Cornwall, England, were flooding into southern Wisconsin to mine lead, referred to as "gray gold" at the time. So many came so fast that houses were scarce, and many miners survived the harsh winters by living in tunnels burrowed into the hillsides, not unlike how native badgers faced the winter. Soon the human cave dwellers were nicknamed "badgers," and the moniker stuck, with Wisconsin being called the Badger State ever since.

Concurrently, American traders were flooding into the Milwaukee area to take over and enlarge the trade once dominated by the British. In short order, farmer-settlers started moving in, claiming the land as their own personal property. By 1832 white settlers were sparring over land rights with the native inhabitants, and farmers were happy to hear that Chief Black Hawk had rebelled against the US government and was being pursued into Wisconsin by six hundred soldiers and about ten times that many militiamen. Black Hawk and his Sauk tribe had never agreed to the Treaty of Saint Louis, and he believed that the land around Rock River, Illinois, was his tribe's birthright, that it had been guaranteed to them by the US government for "as long as they like," and that they had an iron-clad agreement with that government for a perpetual right to these lands "to enjoy them, hunting, planting, and dwelling thereon, so long as they please, without any molestation from the United States." When he crossed the Mississippi with his followers and marched to Rock River, Illinois, the settlers there had a different idea. After a few skirmishes, the US army began a pursuit north that forced Black Hawk into Wisconsin Territory. A solid defeat of Black Hawk's men would be the final straw needed to push the Sauk and Winnebago across the Mississippi River, leaving what would soon become the state of Wisconsin open season fo land-seeking settlers. Most of the land was relatively flat, and all of it was covered with rich black soil. Farmers poured into the territory, stimulating the government to officially create the "Wiskonsin" Territory on April 20, 1836. Shortly thereafter, increased use of the steamboat to transport goods up and down the Mississippi River demanded refueling sites along the less-appealing river bluffs, encouraging another wave of immigrants.

By the mid-1840s, the population of the Wisconsin territory had increased to over 150,000—twice the number required to become a state. Interestingly, the first constitution created was considered too progressive (for example, it allowed women to own property) by the general public, and a more restrictive constitution had to be written before the citizens approved, thereby enabling Wisconsin to become a state on May 29, 1848. Wisconsin was the thirtieth state to join the Union and the last territory east of the Mississippi River to become a state.

About ten years after the US government seized the last land east of the Mississippi River occupied by the Winnebago, which it had done around 1837, settlers began to move into the area north of Bad Ax River.[3] The first

---

[3] When N. E. Whiteside, assisted by chainmen U. Gales and A. L. Eaton and marker A. Hetzler, surveyed Townships 12 and 13 north, range 7 west (aka Genoa) in the first quarter of 1816, he concluded about township 12: "This township is measurably unfit for cultivation, being hilly and broken. Soil mostly third rate and poor. In general, the timber is of an inferior growth of burr, white and black oak. The hills fronting the Mississippi and Bad Ax rivers are in places entirely shorn of vegetation, covered with rock, flint and iron rust. It is in all parts well supplied with springs of finest quality. The bottom of Bad Ax river (although wider in this township than any place else), is limited and mostly low and wet. The Mississippi river above and below the mouth

known patent for a partial section of land in Bad Ax (Genoa) Township was granted to Albert Whitman Pariss on February 24, 1848.

Before Genoa was Genoa it was Bad Ax City, and before that it was called Hastings Landing. When the potential village became incorporated on January 9, 1849, the founders gave the town the name of Bad Ax City and the surrounding area Bad Ax Township. Wisconsin had been a state for less than nine months. At the time, Bad Ax Town was part of Crawford County. On March 1, 1851, Crawford County was divided; the southern third kept the name, the northern third became La Crosse County, and the middle county adopted the name Bad Ax County (total county population about 700). Stephen Pedretti, Adelaide Lombardi, John Venner, Mary Ann Buzzetti, Bartholomew Starlochi, Mary Zabolio-Starlochi and Mary Madeleine Starlochi immigrated to Bad Ax City, a part of Bad Ax Township located in Bad Ax County. Can you imagine leaving the comfort of Prestone, a quiet subdivision of Campodolcino and San Bernardo, to move to a place thrice named Bad Ax? All these Bad Axes took their name from Bad Ax River, which has kept the name (though changed the spelling to Bad Axe). No one knows why the Mississippi River tributary got that name, but we do know that early French settlers called it "la mauvaise hache" and that the name stuck.

---

of Bad Ax, has little or no bottom, bounded by a perpendicular ledge of sandstone, ranging from 3 to 10 chains (200 to 660 feet) from the river and falling abruptly from the base of the perpendicular, to the water's edge, covered with large tumbling rocks, scattering burr, white and black oak trees" (*History of Vernon County, Wisconsin*, p. 113).

The author of the *History of Vernon County, Wisconsin* has a more interesting and elaborate story of the name's origin:

In 1851 the counties of Bad Ax and La Crosse were organized from portions of the territory of Crawford. In what manner Bad Ax County got its name, no one seemed to know. Some contended that the name was a corruption of the French word bateaux [boats]; that some French trader loaded *bateaux* with goods to trade to the Indians for furs, and that he anchored his boats at the mouth of the Bad Ax River, and established a trading post there; that the Indians could not say *bateaux*; that the nearest they could come to the pronunciation of the word, was *badax*, and that thus the name of Bad Ax got fastened on the river, and the river gave the name to the county. I do not know how correct this theory may be, one thing is certain, the waters of that river have ever been cool, clear and sparkling, and bright, and the trout that darted through its crystal waters, very large, lively fellows, and of superior flavor. That stream deserves a better name. Another theory of the older settlers was that in the long, long ago, when Prairie du Chien was nothing but a French trading post, a trader loaded his *bateaux* with goods of various kinds to trade to the Indians for furs; that he, too, moored his boats near the mouth of the Bad Ax, and that he had, among other articles, a large quantity of axes which he traded off to the Indians; that the axes all proved to be *bad*, worthless, and that the trader and the river near whose mouth he traded, got the name of Bad Ax, and the latter gave the name to the county. These traditions will probably soon be lost, and the origin of the name will be concealed in eternal mystery.

But whatever may have been the origin of the name, it was, from the first, a blight to the county, although the old pioneers seemed to be a long while in learning the fact. What has even been a source of wonder to me, is, that the Legislature of the State ever gave such a name to the county, but after it was done, successive Legislatures seemed to take delight in making fun of it and of its inhabitants. For many years the Legislature held annually what was called a "Session of the Sovereigns," the whole thing being a huge burlesque, and in those sessions, in one form or another Bad Ax would be wrung in. On such occasions, the "Gentleman from *Bad Acts*," would figure conspicuously.

It is a fact that letters came to the post office in Viroqua with the figures of broken, bruised, battered, bent, and twisted axes preceding the word county, thus by caricature indicating the county in which Viroqua was located. . . . The name was retarding the settlement of the county. Still, many of the old pioneers seemed to like the name, and were satisfied with it. There were those who thought the very oddity of the name would attract settlers. There were young people growing up all around to whose ears the name Bad Ax sounded uncouth, and I knew the sturdy pioneer would have to bend to "young

America." In 1861 Judge Terhune came one day with
a petition to the Legislature asking that the name be
changed to Vernon, and with a bill that he had
drawn making the change. The bill was well and
carefully drawn, and bill and petition were sent to
Gov. Rusk, who then represented one of the
Assembly districts in Bad Ax County in the
Legislature. He at once introduced the bill; it was
soon passed, approved and became a law, and the
name Bad Ax went into—not oblivion,
unfortunately, but "into the flood of things that are
past"—at least so far as applicable to the county. But
there was even then too much Bad Ax in the county:
there was Bad Ax City (now Genoa), Bad Ax
postoffice (now Liberty Pole), and the Bad Ax river.
All have passed away but the river, and let that
remain—it is a romantic remembrance of the past.
(pp. 228–229)

The most prominent "romantic remembrance of the
past" was the Battle of Bad Ax in 1832, in which a US
militia—mostly volunteers—put an end to the Black Hawk
War by cornering the woman and children following Black
Hawk between the mouth of the Bad Ax River and the
Mississippi. Black Hawk had tried to surrender on more
than one occasion, and when that failed was leading his
followers toward the Mississippi in order to cross to the
west side, which is what the US government proclaimed was
their goal. Instead of accepting Black Hawk's offer to
surrender, neither assisting nor even allowing his crossing
to west banks, they sent a gunboat up from Prairie du Chien
ɔ cut off the retreat. The warriors, trying to make sure their

helpless women and children would not be harmed, attempted to divert the militia. While some soldiers followed the warriors, others cornered the defenseless. Motivated by fear and hatred, the deputy soldiers and enlisted soldiers hunted down the starving and defenseless prey and slaughtered them in cold blood as they attempted to swim across the Mississippi River. Caught between the gunboat and the soldiers on the east bank, the defenseless Sauk women and children were massacred. It is instructive to read commentary written by the pursuers as they describe heroically wading through marshland up to their armpits and bramble so thick they can barely make a few miles a day, in desperate pursuit of the dangerous "savages" (remember, they had attempted to surrender numerous times) and the glee expressed as they mowed them down when the hunt ended—with the victims within easy shooting range. Shortly thereafter the male warriors, including Black Hawk, were arrested, and the last battle to be fought between natives and invaders east of the Mississippi was over.

After this battle, immigrants flooded into Wisconsin territory. William Henry Harrison was elected president of the United States, and General Dodge, one of the leaders of the massacre at Bad Ax, became the first territorial governor of Wisconsin and then was elected twice to serve as Wisconsin's first US senator. Abraham Lincoln, a member of one of the militias that pursued Black Hawk (but who never saw battle), was elected the sixteenth president of the United States. Black Hawk spent some time as a refuge, then a prisoner, and finally as a spokesman for cooperation between whites and Sauk. His book, *Th*

Autobiography of Ma-Ka-Tai-Me-She-Kia-Kiak, or Black Hawk, Embracing the Traditions of His Nation, Various Wars in Which He Has Been Engaged, and His Account of the Cause and General History of the Black Hawk War of 1832, His Surrender, and Travels through the United States. Also Life, Death and Burial of the Old Chief, Together with a History of the Black Hawk War, was published in 1833 and became a best seller.

It was in 1853, just twenty years after the Battle of Bad Ax, when Joseph Monti received a patent for land in sections 28 and 29 that he divided into twenty-one blocks (three were partial blocks) each with eight plats per block to be sold to immigrants to build homes or businesses in his envisioned village, now called Bad Ax after the only river flowing through the township.

Later in the year, Bartholomew Starlocki arrived with his family and purchased a lot on the west side of Main Street, where he had a cement-block home built in 1856 for his family. He also purchased nearly a dozen forty-acre plats spread across the township. His property was valued at over $500.00 by 1855, according to Ernesto R. Milani in his 2004 paper (p. 8). Starlochi's home was the site of the first Catholic Mass held in Genoa and is believed to have been a funeral Mass for his mother, Maria Teresa Domenica P. Buzzetti, who passed away on September 10, 1862. That home stood for well over seventy-five years before it was demolished. The Catholic residents organized Saint Charles parish that year and by 1864 had built a small wooden church at the site where the current Catholic church stands.

You can understand why the gentle souls coming from Campodolcino wanted to change the name of the town.

According to Patricia Harrsch in *Civil Towns of Wisconsin*, the name of the city was changed from Bad Ax City to Lockhaven on March 28, 1857. However, other sources cited by the Wisconsin Historical Society state that the county legislature gave the name Genoa to the town on November 12, 1861:

> On the first day of the [county legislature] session the board created a new town under the name of Genoa. On the 12th of November, 1861, the town of Genoa was created. The territory embraced by Genoa is probably best described by tracing the boundaries, commencing at the southwest corner of section 16, township 12, range 6 west, thence south of the west line of the town of Sterling to the northeast corner of section 29, township 12, range 6 west, thence west on the section line to the Mississippi river, thence up the river to the north line of section 19, township 13, range 7, thence east on the section line to the northeast corner of section 24, township 13, range 7, thence south on the line to the township line between townships 12 and 13, thence east along that line to the northeast corner of section 5, township 12, range 6 west, thence south to the place of beginning. (*History of Vernon County, Wisconsin*, p. 144)

A feature story appearing in the *La Crosse Tribune & Leader Press* on July 21, 1938, stated that prior to 1868, the city was called Bad Ax City. This seems to be based on a statement in another section of the *History of Vernon County*: "For a time it was thought the name Bad Ax quite appropriate as the people were for years kept in fear, by the bad characters that constantly infested their vicinity, from off the Mississippi River, as it was quite a steam-boat landing for steamers plying up and down the river. However, in 1868, the people thought the name had a tendency to keep the town from being settled by the better class of people, and hence they changed the name" (p. 531).

All these things could be true. Some people living there, unhappy with the charming name of Bad Ax City, could have started calling their home town Lockhaven; the fathers of the city could have petitioned the county who officially acknowledged the name of the township as Genoa in 1861; but the village continued to be called Bad Ax City by the public and the press for a few years, until 1868 when they proclaimed the village should also be called Genoa. There is no working theory on why the residents chose Genoa. No one was from Genoa, Italy; no one had sailed from Genoa, and apparently no one living in Bad Ax at the time the name changed had ever been in Genoa, Italy. Some claim it was to honor Christopher Columbus, who was born in Genoa, Italy. That seems a stretch. We do know that in 1861 the majority of the people living in Bad Ax were Italian immigrants from Val San Giacomo and Airolo. We know that they chose an Italian name. We also know that many immigrants in this era named their new towns after their home-country towns, sometimes by putting new in front of the name. New Campodolcino would certainly have made more sense than Genoa. Many were from Campodolcino, and the name means "field of sweetness." These fields of rich black soil were certainly sweet discoveries for our newly settled immigrants. Why not that name? Old rivalries may have surfaced. After all, there were as many immigrants from Starleggia, Francesco, Airolo, Vho, and San Bernardo as there were from Campodolcino. At the time, Bad Ax was a vibrant river port. Back home, Genoa was a vibrant port. Genoa, Italy, got its name because the water bends like a knee to form a perfect seaport. At that time the Mississippi bent like a knee to form the Genoa port. It is probably too much to suppose there was a linguist that knew Genoa, genuflect, genus, and genuine evolved from the Latin word for knee, *genua*. These were genuine tight-knit people who often genuflected to thank God for their blessings and who benefited from that bend in the river that made their new home a natural port, which had originally attracted them to the area. I should note here that the word *genuine* originally described the sincere feeling that Romans felt for their offspring when they bounced them on their knees (genua). Genoa was just the right name if the citizens could not agree on New Campodolcino or Saint Bernard as the name to replace Bad Ax City.

The people of Genoa, Wisconsin, do not pronounce the name of the town the way other Americans do. They do not say "GEN-o-a" but "ge-NO-a." "Ge" is pronounced like the first sound in Jehovah and "noa" like Noah. This pronunciation comes from Val San Giacomo dialect and would have been how Genoa was pronounced at the time in Val San Giacomo.

Shortly after renaming their community, the Catholic residents organized Saint Charles parish and by 1864 had built a small wooden church at the site where the current Catholic church stands. Soon there were two clamshell button factories, a lumber yard, and several operating limestone quarries. In 1877 Albert Zabolio and his father

Augustine built a dry goods and general store that would serve as a hub for the town for the next one hundred years. Albert married his second cousin Rosa Starlochi in 1882. Their son Adolph and his two sons Albert and Edward kept the store alive until 1986. In 1884 the Chicago, Burlington & Northern Railroad completed its route through Genoa. It offered freight and passenger service for the residents and gave the village a faster and less expensive way to sell and purchase goods and access to the rest of the country, especially to the services available in the larger city of La Crosse. The new trade opportunities led to the building of Latimer Sons Dealers General Merchandise, a second grocery and dry goods store, and more inns and taverns.

There is a strong possibility that the land purchased by the Pedretti, Vener, Sterlocchi, and Buzzetti families was part of the 500,000 acres of land granted to Wisconsin by the federal government to raise funds for public schools, for much of Bad Ax County was land-grant acreage. The desire to have their children educated could have been part of the motivation for these immigrants to settle in a land-grant state.

By 1868 Genoa Township was fully settled, with 683 people living in 130 dwellings, only slightly less populated than the year 2000 when the census reported there were 705 people, 285 households, and 196 families residing in the township. The story of these early years might be best told through the words of the authors of the 1884 *History of Vernon County, Wisconsin*.

The preface to the book states: "Believing that the county of Vernon afforded material for a good history, the Union Publishing Company of Springfield, Illinois, sent a corps of experienced historians into the field under the supervision of Prof. C. W. Butterfield with instructions to spare no pains in compiling a complete and reliable work." The result of their effort, the *History of Vernon County, Wisconsin, Together with Sketches of Its Towns, Villages and Townships, Educational, Civil, Military and Political History; Portraits of Prominent Persons, and Biographies of Representative Citizens*, was published in 1884. Genoa figures prominently throughout the book, and chapter 36 (pages 527–535) is devoted to the history of the township and village. Matthew Monti and William L. Riley certified that all information in the book pertaining to Genoa and especially in chapter 36 was accurate and that they "made such additions and corrections, as we in our judgment, deem necessary, and that as corrected, we to the best of our recollection, consider it a true history and approve of the same."

I will include here several selections from the book, as it is one of the earliest written documents covering the first thirty years of Euro-American occupation of Genoa Township. These authors were close in time to the reporting, and for the most part their facts can be trusted. Recent research shows some facts to be inaccurate even on such a simple matter of spelling names consistently; for example, these three spellings are all for the same family name: Zabolie, Zabolio, and Zabolia. From today's perspective, the information included seems oddly selective. For example, there is no mention of prominent citizens Bart Starlochi and Joe Morelli, or that Fred Morelli and Albert Schubert ran a blacksmith shop. Keeping in mind there are some errors in facts presented and conspicuous gaps of missing information for no apparent reason, I present for your reading pleasure the following excerpts:

"The first settler was William Tibbitts, who entered 160 acres of land on section 22, in 1850. He was followed the same year by Elias Shisler, who entered 120 acres of land on section 22, where he was still living in 1884."

"This village was laid out and platted by Joseph Monti, on section 28, in the year 1854, and was first named Bad Ax, after the only river in the town of Genoa. For a time it was thought the name Bad Ax quite appropriate as the people were for years kept in fear, by the bad characters that constantly infested their vicinity, from off the Mississippi River, as it was quite a steam-boat landing for steamers, plying up and down the river. However, in 1868, the people thought the name had a tendency to keep the town from being settled by the better class of people, and hence they changed the name. The original plat of the village contained twenty-one blocks. Block 12 was donated to the public, for public uses, by Joseph Monti, and afterward became the public square."

"The first house was erected by David Hastings, in 1853."

"John Ott, one of the wealthiest farmers of the town of Genoa, entered forty acres of land on section 34, in 1853."

"A hotel was erected in 1854 by Sylvester Lupi."

"The first birth of a white child was J. W., son of Samuel and Martha Kelsie, in 1854."

"Genoa postoffice was established in 1854, on section 29, on the site of the village of Genoa. The first postmaster was Jacob Kelsie, who was after a time succeeded by James McGrath, Mathew Monti, Wm. Bullock and J. B. Bozola, who was postmaster in 1884. Romance postoffice was established in 1854, on section 6. The first postmaster was John Tewalt. He was succeeded by William Fox, who still held the office in 1884."

"Ferdinand Guscatte settled where Genoa now stands, in 1855, and engaged in the manufacture of wagons."

"The first school was taught in 1855 in a log house, afterward used for a hotel."

"The first school in the town of Genoa was taught by Sarah A Bacus, in 1855, on section 28."

"The first school was taught by Sarah A. Bacus, in 1856." (Note contradiction.)

"The first couple married in the town of Genoa, was David Hastings and Miss Kelsie, in 1856."

"The first death in the town was David Hastings, in 1856."

"The first religious services were held at the residence of Samuel Kelsie, by Rev. Delap, in 1856."

"To the Newton circuit G. W. Nuzum was appointed first minister in the year 1856 and he made his place of residence the village of Newton, situated on the Bad Ax River. His places of preaching were Newton, Springville, Bad Ax City (now Genoa) and several private dwellings." (Nuzum was a preacher for the Methodist Episcopal Conference.)

"William Stephenson came in 1856 and purchased eighty acres of land on section 17, where he was still living in 1884."

"Charles Brown came the same year (1856), and entered forty acres of land on section 20."

"John Fopper came in 1857 and settled on section 28, of which he purchased eighty acres."

"The first saw mill was built by William Officer, in 1858."

"Maj. N. W. Hamilton was one of the settlers of 1858. He was born in Fayette Co., Ind., in 1820, and settled in the town of Jefferson, this county, in 1854, where he entered land which he afterward sold to Ramsey and Miller, and then entered eighty acres of land in the town of Genoa, on section 4, moving there in 1858. Mr. Hamilton was married to Alnudia Clark, in 1853, by whom he has four children— Emla, Isabell, Irila and Jenett. He was the first school treasurer of the town of Genoa, and held the office for eleven years."

"The first election of what is known as the town of Genoa was held April 7, 1860, at the village school house of Genoa. The first officers were: E. Page, chairman, Peter Shumway and Willis Masker, supervisors; William Burlock, clerk; John Greeman, treasurer; Willis Masker, assessor. Officers of 1883: William Riley, chairman, William Hall and August Vegline, supervisors; Mathew Monti, clerk; Barnard Gadola, treasurer; John Carpenter, assessor."

"The first school house was built, in 1860, on section 28, where the village of Genoa now stands."

"The St. Charles Catholic Church was organized in 1862, and a church edifice erected two years later, in the village of Genoa. This building was 24x36 feet, and cost $500. The Church was organized by Rev. Father Marko."

"In 1884 the Church numbered about 300."

"In 1884 the town (township) contained six school buildings, valued at $2,200. The town at this date had a school population of 37."[4]

"The business of the place [Genoa] in 1884 was represented as follows: Mathew Monti and Albert Zabolio, dealers in dry goods, boots, shoes, crockery and hardware."

"J. P. Monti, proprietor of the only hotel."

"Albert Guscetti, blacksmith and wagon shop."

"There were two cemeteries within the town of Genoa, in 1884. One situated a half mile from Bad Ax city (Genoa), on land owned at an early day by Samuel Kelsie, on section 21. The other burying place was on section 28" (pp. 530, 531).

"The only religious societies in Genoa, in 1884, was that of the Roman Catholic, who organized at an early day. This Church is made up largely of Italians. Other denominations have held meetings from time to time at school houses."

Chapter 36 also presents several short biographies of Genoa residents. Only four are of interest to our story. I present them in whole:

> Mathew Monti, a son of Joseph Monti, the founder of the village of Genoa, and its present postmaster [not in agreement with above statement], was born in New York City in 1840. His father was a native of Switzerland, born in 1811, and

---

[4] In the edition I consulted, the number appears to have a smeared 5 between the 3 and 7. It would not have been possible to have 357 students with a total population of less than 690 residents, so I am concluding the number reported was 37.

immigrated to the United States in 1832, locating in New York City. Mr. Monti's mother was born in Philadelphia, Penn., in 1811, and died in Vernon Co., Wis., in 1880. When Mr. Monti was but a year old his parents moved to Cincinnati, Ohio, and in 1842 to St. Louis, Mo.; thence to Galena, Ill., where they resided until 1863. In 1853 Mr. Joseph Monti came to Vernon County and entered 296 acres of land in the town of Genoa. Being of an enterprising disposition he laid out and platted the village of Bad Ax (now Genoa), which he named after the county of Bad Ax (now Vernon). Mr. Mathew Monti now owns twenty acres of land on section 28 and village property. In 1882 he engaged in mercantile pursuits and now owns a stock of goods valued at $2,000 [more than $50,000 in 2016 dollars]. Mr. Monti has served his neighbors and citizens as clerk of the school district six years, justice of the peace ten years; was also town treasurer and has been town clerk and postmaster of Genoa for seven years. He was united in marriage in 1864 to Almira Greenman and three children have been born to them—Leona, Augustus and Blanche.

William S. Riley, one of the well known citizens of the town of Genoa, was born at Marietta, Ohio, in 1845, and remained there until 1858. In the latter year he came to Vernon Co., Wis., and located at Viroqua. In 1861 he enlisted in Company I, 6th regiment, Wisconsin Volunteer Infantry, and was discharged in 1864. He was captain of the Vernon County Light Guards for two years and under-sheriff for one term. For the past three years Mr. Riley has been chairman of the town board of supervisors. He is a contractor and builder by occupation and has erected some of the finest buildings and residences in Vernon Co. In 1882 Mr. Kiley was married to Anna Lupi. They have one child—Augusta C.

Ferdinand Guscetti, who lives on section 28, came to this town in 1855. He was living in Jo Daviess Co., Ill, and there carried on the manufacture of wagons. At the earnest solicitation of Joseph Monti, of this town, he was induced to come to Genoa and became a settler in 1855. He located in Genoa village when the country around was quite a wilderness and was a wagon maker there for many years. He finally sold his shop and bought eighty-two acres of land on section 28, where he now lives. In 1864 Mr. Guscetti enlisted in the 1st Wisconsin Heavy Artillery and served through the war. He was married in 1840 to Mary Buffi. Of seven children born to them only three are living— Matthew, Juliett, wife of Daniel Biffi, and Catharine.

Albert Zabolie [sic] was born in Italy in 1858, and emigrated [sic] with his parents to the United States in 1877, and settled in the village of Genoa, where his father and himself [sic] opened a dry goods and general store. They now carry the largest stock of goods in the village, valued at about $5,000 [more than $125,000 in 2016 dollars]. Mr. Zabolie was married in 1882 to Rosa Starlochi, of Vernon County. Mr. Zabolie's father, August Zabolie, is still living in the village of Genoa. Albert is doing a prosperous business in his line of trade.

By 1884 most plots of land were occupied, dairy farming had replaced the earlier "wheat" farms, most of the Italians who immigrated to Genoa were well settled, the A. Zabolio Co., a dry goods and hardware store, was well established, and the railway that connected Genoa to Chicago and Minneapolis and beyond was completed.

# # #

More of the Genoa story will be told in Volume 7 of *The Story of Our Stories* - titled *The Diary of an Immigrant: Giovanni Vener.*

Genoa Wisconsin
Circa 1858

The stone house on the upper left was built by Morelli in 1853. The next building, the barnlike building with a fence behind it, is believed to have originally housed the Pedretti brothers. It may have been the home of Stefano Pedretti, his wife, Adelaide Lombardi, and their first four children when this picture was taken. The house in foreground that appears to be made of concrete block was built by Bartholomew Starlochi in 1856 and in 1862 hosted the first Catholic Mass.

The date of the picture is unknown. There is no sign in the picture of the Catholic Church that was built in 1864 (although it could be off to the left of this picture). I believe by 1864 the town would have been more built up, as many immigrants had arrived by then. So I am going to allege this is not a picture of Genoa but of Bad Ax City taken before 1860. You will notice in this picture that the Genoa Bluff has almost no trees on it, and there is what appears to be a pigpen where the entire bluff has since grown back. Also take note of the chickens on the road in front of the house on the left, believed to be the home of the Pedrettis until 1868 when Stephano Pedretti purchased a forty acre plat just east of the city. The first settlers must have cut the trees down for lumber, for their own firewood, and for fuel to sell to the steamboats coming up and down the Mississippi River. But as the town developed, this hillside returned to the forest it is today. The house built by Morelli, known later as the Margaret Gilardi house, is surrounded by trees in a 1930 photo, and the area where the pigpen is shown looked like a forest. When I went to Saint Charles School in the 1950s, the Gilardi House was still occupied, but it was completely hidden behind trees, and the path to the house was an uphill walk, for the road leading up to the church had been made lower than the one you see in this picture.

Mississippi Scenery, Genoa, Wis.

Genoa, Wisconsin

Based on growth of trees, this picture was probably taken about 5 years later. It is believed that the Pedretti brothers and Stefano and Adelaide and their five children lived in the small barn-house in the middle of this picture.

Circa 1864

Genoa Wisconsin
Circa 1875

Genoa Depot

In 1884 the Chicago, Burlington & Northern Railroad completed its route through Genoa. It offered freight and passenger service for the residents and gave the village a faster and less expensive way to sell and purchase goods and access to the rest of the country, especially to the services available in the larger city of La Crosse.

Starlochi home
Built in 1856

This photo of the original Starlochi home was probably taken around 1910. The home was demolished in the 1920s. Later the lot housed a root beer stand and is now the parking lot for the Genoa Bank.

Morelli house

This is copy of a photo that appeared in the La Crosse
Tribune in 1930. At the time the house was occupied by
Margaret Gilardi and was generally referred to as the
Gilardi house up until it crumbled.

Genoa, Wisconsin

Top Photo: Zabolio Dry Goods Store and Monti Hotel

Circa 1880

Genoa, Wisconsin

Circa 1885

GENOA BLACKSMITH SHOP
Photo, 1902

Genoa button factory
Circa 1903
A pearl found in 1903 is reputed to be in the crown of
the Queen of England.

Genoa, Wisconsin circa 1890

Genoa, Wisconsin
2010
Photo by Michela Fanetti taken from atop the Genoa
Bluff

A Call for a New Epic

"I sing of arms and man"
—Virgil, *The Aeneid*

"I sing of kindness and woman"
—Pedretti, *The Story of Our Stories*

It is the spring of 1960 and our senior class has just completed reading Virgil's *The Aeneid* in Latin. Our professor, James Coke, who has walked us through Virgil's insights with love and kindness, opens the dialogue to discuss other epics and their influence on the peoples for whom they were written. He cites among others *The Iliad* and *The Odyssey*, the Bible, *Beowulf*, *The Divine Comedy*, *Paradise Lost*, the Mahabharata, and *The Epic of Gilgamesh*. Each portrayed heroes or creatures of other worlds, larger than life but also deeply flawed, who took on "evil forces" in a multifarious but structured manner that became the common memory of the peoples for whom they spoke. The epics forged for their societies new paradigms that set ethical standards, established limitations that curbed natural freedoms, and loomed with subliminal power over the consciousness of generations to come as the power of their words and stories foreshadowed and triggered events to come. All celebrated the warrior, war, violence, revenge (sometimes disguised as justice), and the ultimate victory of might and the establishment of a privileged class. (These thoughts may more reflect the thinking of an impressionable student than the words of the professor.)

Coke states dogmatically, "No nation can come into its own without its own epic." Then with arrogance, which is quite unlike Professor Coke, he states, leaving little room for discussion, "America will never have an epic as we have no heroes of epic magnitude; we fought no wars that shaped who we are; we have no Junos we believe we can thwart, no enemy worthy of their own epic if they had defeated us. Let's look again at Virgil's opening lines." He reads them aloud to us:

> Arma virumque cano, Troiae qui primus ab oris Italiam, fato profugus, Laviniaque venit litora, multum ille et terris iactatus et alto vi superum saevae memorem Iunonis ob iram; multa quoque et bello passus, dum conderet urbem, inferretque deos Latio, genus unde Latinum, Albanique patres, atque altae moenia Roma.

> Musa, mihi causas memora, quo numine laeso, quidve dolens, regina deum tot volvere casus insignem pietate virum, tot adire labores impulerit. Tantaene animis caelestibus irae?

In translation:

> I sing of arms and of man, first in Italy
> Birthed in Troy, he suffered in war, exiled by fate,
> Cast out a vagabond, he braved the storms on land
> and sea
> On account of the mindful wrath of Juno;
> Until he came to the shores of Lavina,
> Built a city to bring his gods to the Latin genus,

Fathered Alba Longa and the high walls of Rome.
Muse, remind me the grounds the queen god
Felt her power so injured, sensed ongoing disaster,
That pressed her to push this pious man through
    colossal
Trials. Is this the conduct of a heavenly god?
    (Translation by author)

Coke continues, "What American poet could begin with those lines? None." Discussion over.

I think to myself, why does the Great American Epic have to be about warriors and war? Why does today's epic have to be about limiting freedom? The epics of old met the needs of their society. Coke is, or at least should be, right; we will never have that kind of epic.

"I sing of arms and of man." "I celebrate war and the warrior" is an equally good translation. The warrior in this case is Aeneas, and the wars are the bloody battles that allow the Trojan refugee to eventually dominate the native Latins, take the capital city of Rome, and begin the long road of violence and aggression that established the Roman Empire.

Virgil is celebrating war and the bloodletting that comes with war. The hero is male, violent, flawed, victorious, vengeful, larger than life, who lives above the codes that the epic prescribes for the society that, in the end, is to be submissive to the hero and his offspring (in this case Augustus), who are also expected to discount every moral code that defines the society they lead. Does Aeneas mature into a more civilized being? Do his descendants? When does Virgil call for empathy, fairness, or gentleness?

Virgil's epic ends in the cold-blooded revenge-murder

of Turnus perpetrated by Aeneas, the "man" being sung about in the epic, just after he is victorious in taking Rome. He stands over his enemy and considers being compassionate, but when he sees Turnus wearing the belt of Pallas whom Turnus had slain in battle, Aeneas thrusts his sword "deep into his bosom." Virgil's epic ends in the "streaming blood" of the enemy and the glorious victory of arms and man:

> Aeneas volvens oculos dextramque repressit; et iam iamque magis cunctantem flectere sermo coeperat, infelix umero cum apparuit alto balteus et notis fulserunt cingula bullis.

> Pallantis pueri, victum quem vulnere Turnus straverat atque umeris inimicum insigne gerebat. ille, oculis postquam saevi monimenta doloris exuviasque hausit, furiis accensus et ira terribilis: 'tune hinc spoliis indute meorum eripiare mihi? Pallas te hoc vulnere, Pallas immolat et poenam scelerato ex sanguine sumit.' hoc dicens ferrum adverso sub pectore condit fervidus; ast illi solvuntur frigore membra vitaque cum gemitu fugit indignata sub umbras.

Translation by John Dryden:

> And, just prepar'd to strike, repress'd his hand. He roll'd his eyes, and ev'ry moment felt

> His manly soul with more compassion melt; When, casting down a casual glance, he spied

> The golden belt that glitter'd on his side, The fatal spoils which haughty Turnus tore from dying Pallas, and in triumph wore.

Then, rous'd anew to wrath, he loudly cries
(Flames, while he spoke, came flashing from his
        eyes) "Traitor, dost thou, dost thou to grace
        pretend,
Clad, as thou art, in trophies of my friend? To his
        sad soul a grateful off'ring go!
'Tis Pallas, Pallas gives this deadly blow." He rais'd
        his arm aloft, and, at the word, Deep in his
        bosom drove the shining sword.
The streaming blood distain'd his arms around,
And the disdainful soul came rushing thro' the
        wound.

We see the proud and victorious Aeneas, the invader from Troy, stand over Turnus, the leader of the native Latins. Aeneas could have and almost does show compassion and spare the life of the defeated and humiliated Turnus. But revenge rules the day. When Aeneas sees that Turnus is wearing the armor of Aeneas's protégé Pallas, Aeneas raises his sword and thrusts it into Turnus, killing him instantly and spilling his blood and soul on the ground to fertilize centuries of brutality and power known ironically as Pax Romana. The work concludes celebrating revenge, one of human's least honorable traits.

Was Coke right? Is there is no American "hero" that could measure up to the standards of heroism, violence, and revenge established by Homer and Virgil?

George Washington might seem a natural, but American puritanical mythology has turned him into a goody-two-shoes far too frail for a major flaw considered a requirement for a classical epic hero. It is probably impossible for an author to change his reputation from that of a reluctant leader into a powerful (and far more honest) representation of the power-grabbing, egocentric, driven man that he was. Lincoln, too, has been immortalized on hallow grounds much too sacred for an epic hero. Plus, he was far from a military hero. Whitman might do, but it is unlikely Americans would ever take a poet seriously enough, and he was the antithesis of the requisite warrior that Coke and others seem to think is part and parcel of epic heroism. The idea of Jackson, Harrison, Grant, MacArthur, or Eisenhower serving as an epic hero parallel to Aeneas or Ulysses is too funny to even discuss. Benedict Arnold turned traitor. Teddy Roosevelt had the flaws, but his victory was inconsequential. Lee and Jackson lost. Patton was too mean in more than one sense of that word. In addition, few modern readers could be sucked into believing that supernatural heroes existed let alone had some power to impose on the choices we make. Hopefully, today's reader would not revel in cold-blooded murder by a sheriff-judge-jury-and-executioner hero of the classical epic.

Still, it seemed to a young romantic that there was something dead wrong in Coke's proclamation. Most obviously, if a nation could not come of age without an epic to support its perception of itself, and America could never have an epic, then America would never come of age. That seemed an odd prediction for a country that was destined to dominate world politics for generations to come. True, a country that had just elected baby-face JFK and lived through the years of Eisenhower apathy and naiveté looked like it might never reach adolescence, let alone develop a working cultural identity.

Still, most people in the mid-twentieth century predicted world dominance and a short adolescence. (Only fifty years later, the election of a black president and the nomination of a woman for president could symbolize that America was emerging into adulthood as a nation.)

I asked myself, "Does an epic have to celebrate dominance, war, and revenge? Why did an epic have to promote limitation, exclusion, and restriction? Is it not possible to put the historic gentry-sponsored classism, war, violence, and tribalism into the past? Wasn't the American hero the commoner, making things happen by mass commitment rather than individual supremacy? More willing to fight for fair treatment with words than domination by war? More concerned with kindness than control? Capable of letting empathy replace revenge? True, these traits of the American psyche had been obfuscated by writers and songsters, politicians, and economists supported by clergy and educators who were still letting the idea of the plutocratic way of life seduce them into believing it was the only paradigm of progress.

Wasn't the mandate for a great epic the call to identify and celebrate who the people are and what their potential is? The Great American Epic will not honor militaristic, chauvinist warmongers that the press and politicians love but the story of a gentle people, a benevolent people, who believe in the value of all humans and the necessity of fairness to rule supreme. True, we are still a young people and easily duped; we are prey to the privileged propaganda. We almost always substitute revenge for justice, justice for equality, and equality for fairness; we naively have been convinced we can do good with arms when we know that fairness and impartial concern is the order of the day. Yes, we continue to seek heroes by superimposing "heroism" on men who play silly but violent sports games, fight illegal wars, and show their photogenic faces on the big screen, but deep down we know that the hero in our culture is our neighbor and her family. While we, from time to time, idolize the woman next door, we are still not convinced that she holds the present and the future in her hands, that she is who we are, that she represents what we can become far more than Reagan, Bush, Clinton, or Obama—and a zillion times more than O.J., A-Rod, Dr. J, Liberace, Madonna, Mr. T, or Oprah. We know, even as we worship those icons, that it is the verity made in their image that is the big lie—that it is what continues to keep us in our place, distracting us from both reaching beyond our self-imposed limitations and from finding in ourselves the power to transform, to leave war and violence behind us, to forge a future free of nationalism, religion, and weapons of destruction. We have the wherewithal to drive starvation, violence, murder, war, and crimes against humanity to relics of the past, to let them join human sacrifice, slavery, and medieval torture as inconceivable practices once proudly perpetrated by humans on humans. If a national epic can bring a people to their potential, the real but hidden America was crying out for that epic to be written. And maybe, just maybe, the task was mine.

For fifty years that challenge stayed with me, alive, nibbling at my heart and soul and from time to time my brain. Along the way I had some realizations. The American epic hero would be a planter—one who planted and cultivated. Our hero had no power or desire to steal the work of others. This insight was followed by an awareness that our hero could not come from the privileged class, by definition a people who rely on others' plantings. Our story was not the story—could not be the story—of someone indulging in the unjust wealth born of others' labor.

As I traveled through life and the world over, I kept an eye out for that hero but did not find him. I wondered, in fact, if he even existed; for a long time I thought Whitman was the rightful American epic hero; I also seriously considered my grandfather and Elvis. All three are heroes, for sure, but not the epic hero I needed to inspire and make a story. I tested Jeannette Rankin, but her story never sparked into a word; for a while I determined that Toni Morrison seemed a natural—a giant among humans, a great woman, the archetypal American success—but it was not the American dream that would provide the skeleton for our epic. In a prequel, my mother was a promising candidate. I got a novel out of her life story—but not an epic by any definition. There was a clown that seemed right. She seemed perfect, and I found the idea of a clown hero full of potential. I could not find the first word to start the story for I could not overcome my biased predisposition that I would have to defend for my readers that a clown hero was inherently right. To defend is to discredit.

Only when I stopped looking did I find that the model for our epic hero had always been in my own backyard—a place that appeared to be an isolated little community of self-sufficient partisans who appeared to know of love only how to withhold it and of hope only that it was for the next life. Their faith was deep but had no breadth; it was a faith in Jesus and what they believed to be his church. They rarely demonstrated anything except the local party line. At best they planted seeds on their farms, nourished them into growing, providing sustenance for many more. At worst, they seemed myopic and parochial. But, as the saying goes, appearances can be deceiving.

When I was five or six years old, I could see that my grandfather Peter Pedretti was a man wise well beyond his eighty-eight years. As I said, at one point I thought he might be the prototype for my epic hero. But he seemed more the exception than the exemplar. I also sensed a force hovering around, under, over, and inside the people who called home the bluffs and coulees along the east side of the Mississippi River just a few miles north of the place some had decided earlier would divide Minnesota from Iowa. I attributed that gut feeling to some false chauvinism about where I was raised. Don't we all think there is both something special and something disparaging about the place we called home in our formative years?

I knew little about these people, where they came from and why they populated this tiny spot, which seemed a great distance even from the middle of nowhere. I visited late in the end of the last century and discovered a gentle people, a caring people. While pausing for a moment to admire a quality I had not known I had left behind, one of my double first cousins interrupted me to ask me if I knew that Jim and Jean and a few others had unearthed a rich history of the two families that merged in the second quarter of the twentieth century to produce thirty-seven members of my generation (more if you count those stillborn or who died within days of birth) who share the same four grandparents, making us more siblings than cousins. At first, family curiosity piqued my interest. Soon I was deep into the search for more detail, more generations of ancestors, more insight into what made us who we are.

While returning from my first trip to the ancestral grounds of my family, I realized that the great American hero I had been seeking for half a century was this family. The hero had been too close (my family) and too far away (family instead of individual) for me to see. Our epic would be about us—you and me. The characters would be our mother and our father, their parents and the parents of their parents. I say "our" instead of "my" because our mothers have always been the planters, the nourishers, the seekers of kindness. It is she who planted seeds, nourished the growth, and fed humanity spiritually, mentally, and corporeally. No matter if the seed was the germ of a plant, an idea, a creative impulse, or a scientific discovery, our mothers planted the seed in rich fertile soil and cultivated, fed, and mothered it into nourishment for others. They never were serfs, never slaveholders, never hoarders, never violent, never warmongers, never greed-worshippers or witch hunters. They were kind, empathic, and generous. They were there when needed and never there when a bother. It was they, not the landed gentry of Virginia nor the elite Bostonians, who were America. It is they, not the czars of corporate America nor the weasels of Wall Street, who are America. It is they, not the lecturers of Ivy League nor the wily of Washington, who are America. It is they that are the future world citizen.

Their story is your story. Their story is the story of every human on earth who dreams of and struggles for freedom, forbearance, and fairness. Their story is the story of every planter of seeds that was ever born: the planter of tomato seeds, of lilac roots, of idea seeds, of creation seeds, of discovery seeds, of fantasy seeds, of day dreamer seeds. Their story is not only the American Epic; their story is the story the Great World Epic.

They know that first they and each of us must ask afresh, "What does it mean to be human?" Without that question, "What does it mean to be American? Female? Jew? Black? Lutheran? Straight?" are simple absurdities.

The Story of Our Stories, filled with many stories, is one story—the story of champions as ingrained in kindness, empathy, generosity, and life as those warrior heroes of past epics were ingrained in force, appetite, war, and death. We celebrate the fruit of the planters of seeds; our precursors celebrated the demolition of bearers of arms.

My friend, you and I are no more prepared to worship warmongers than we are to look up to the gods of Olympia who constantly badgered the heroes of the warrior day. Come with me; listen to the story of our story, the stories of you and me—of our parents, their parents, and their parents and grandparents—of our children and their children and their grandchildren. It is a story of planters, nurturers of advance, and tillers of nutrition, fairness, and inspiration. It is our epic, and it will haunt us until we sack the wagers of war, the supporters of starvation, the manufacturers of munitions, the bigots of nation-states, and the advocates of Abrahamism who prefer killing to devotion, doctrine to freedom, and authority to fairness.

Come, join me:

Versus Aeneidic
I sing of kindness and of woman, first in life,

Birthed in the Valley of Saint James, always
  humbled
Ceaselessly derided, she spirited west
To teeming land nourished
A thousand years by the sons and
Daughters of Turtle.
Afflicted by the relentless fury of the great god
  Misogyny
Still she laid bare the moat of harmony.
Reader, remind me of the grounds the sons
Felt their power so tattered; their soul so empty,
That pressed them to push our mother through
  colossal
Trials. Is this the conduct of a righteous heir?
Trodden under the might of the Sons of Misogyny
Those ministers of misery who maltreated our
  mothers
Turning brother against sister, husband against
  wife,
Parent against child, mother against mother,
Priests indulging souls for tolls; peddling passports
  to heaven,
Soldiers razing for safekeeping none sought,
Lords deflowering virgins by the bushel,
Gods unable or unwilling to speak.
Deceived, molested, ravished, ignored, pillaged
Our mother would not be ground into retaliation
Who had long since left the shores
Of craving, supremacy and war;
Planting wistful prairies of sustenance.
She spoke, "Poet, why are you silent? Write the

words
For you have what it takes
You have heard the stories
Of your mothers and all await your verses.
Sing in clarity; listen to the mothers:
'Starvation is as necessary as the King of France,
Craving as dear as Ubu Roi,
Supremacy as acceptable as the Tsar of Russia,
Self-righteousness as tenable as the world is flat,
Arrogance as useful as the British aristocracy.
Let war and murder be impossible
As human sacrifice and Holokautein is impossible,
Let Jihad join witch hunting,
Revolution become unfashionable,
Nationalism writhe in its own provincialism,
Weapons join the woolly mammoth.'"
Come reader, join our mothers . . .

An Essay

I intend to include at least one essay in each volume that promotes a way of life or point of view that I believe the heroes described in The Story of Our Stories would have favored if they were alive today. I am starting off this series with a proposal written in 2013 that would greatly improve how we handle social security and eventually guarantee every citizen a living income upon retirement. Later volumes will include a detailed essay on epic literature, proof that trinities (not dualities or singularities) rule the universe, a proposal to end war and famine, and a truly short history of humanity, to name a few. The essays are meant to further shape the meaning of our epic.

Creating a SAVE Trust

We can all agree that investing early is the intelligent way to assure a viable retirement, that we should diversify our investments, that it is foolish to invest in a plan that promises long-term, consistent, unrealistic returns, and that no one who has contributed to a retirement fund for all or most of their life should end up receiving little or nothing in return. I'd like to think we could also agree that workers should not be unfairly penalized for making a contribution to our society, that taxes should be allocated in an equitable manner, and that every American after a life of contributing to the country through work, social service, military service, raising a family, and so on deserves and needs to be able to retire with a guaranteed income. What could be more devastating than to tell our citizens we intend to turn them out to pasture on wasteland when they retire after making numerous contributions to our society?

Most experts agree that the current Social Security system in America is headed for an implosion.[1] Three realities underlie and undermine today's Social Security system in America: 1) the wage tax is an extreme regressive tax; 2) the distribution of benefits, while seemingly favoring the poor, has paid out much larger, completely subsidized benefit checks to the wealthy; and 3) the system's success to date requires today's investors to pay for yesterday's investors. To put it more directly, today's taxpayers are not putting away for their old age but are paying for today's retirees, and the wealthy have and continue to put in a scandalously small portion while extracting an extremely high return from the Social Security trust fund. There is no doubt the current approach is headed for bankruptcy, for no social arrangement can last indefinitely that extracts from the poor in order to provide unrealistic returns to the wealthy.

To be sure, revenues into the Social Security fund in the seventy-five years between 1937 and 2012 exceeded expenditures in sixty-four of those years. That is an impressive record. In theory, this could go on forever, with the fund running a small surplus over obligations. In fact, it will not go on forever as investment plans that promise long-term, consistently unrealistic returns end much sooner than expected. Maybe benefits will not end in thirty years, or even one hundred years, but without doubt they will end. At some future date the government will not be able to back up its promise to pay a return for FICA (payroll deduction) "investments" for Americans when they get too old to work.

Do we want to leave the last payees coming to retirement age holding the bag? Imagine that it is you. You spent the better part of your life contributing to a retirement fund with the expectation that you would be able to collect a stipend in your golden years. Instead, for whatever reason, the fund disappears, and you are left with broken promises and the likelihood of starvation as your reward for a life of contribution to the fund and to the country. Do you want that to happen to you? Do you want it to happen to your grandchildren or great-grandchildren? Under the current system, it will happen at some point in the future; of that we can be 100 percent sure.

The Social Security program had begun with balances that made it look like people were actually paying their own way. (At the end of 1940, for example, the fund had 32.8 times as much as it had paid out that year; by 1951 that was down to 7.9 times; by 1967 there was just over one year's surplus; and by the end of 1983 the balance was less than two months of payouts.) According to JusttheFacts website, "For workers who earned average wages and retired at the age of 65 in 1980, it took 2.8 years of receiving old-age benefits to recover the value of their payroll taxes (including interest)." After that, they received a *free*, no-strings-attached benefit check from the Social Security fund.

Clearly, workers were not investing in their retirement benefits but paying for current retirees. No recipient was getting back what they had put in[2]—it had been used years before to pay for their elders' benefits. They were receiving benefits from payments made by current payees. Is it not obvious why the fund is in danger?

The purpose of this commentary is to offer a reasonable and surprisingly inexpensive method to prevent future retirees (who believed they would have some security in return for years of hard work, service to their country, and high payroll taxes) being left with nothing, and to provide a more equitable way to pay for the benefits as well as a more justifiable way to distribute benefits.

First, let's take a closer look at the system as it reached its first full cycle of retirees who had been paying in for the full thirty years (1937–1966) then used to base benefits. Everyone who contributed the maximum during the first thirty years of Social Security would have paid in $2,232 that would have been matched by his or her employer, for a total contribution of $4,464. With a 3.5 percent compounded interest on that investment, the value at retirement would have been less than $6,000. Upon retirement, all who paid in $2,232 received a minimum of $168 per month or $2,016 per year (more if the taxpayer had a spouse or qualifying children). In just over three years, those funds were exhausted, and from then on the retiree received a 100 percent free grant from the Social Security fund, paid for by those still in the workforce. People paying less than the maximum ran out of their annuity even sooner and also began to receive a free grant.

After exhausting his benefits, Mr. Better-paid continued to receive the maximum benefit of $168 per month (more if there was a spouse or qualifying children). If Mr. Better-paid lived until he was 79.6 years old, which was life expectancy of a 65-year-old in 1967[3], he received a grand total of $29,500[4] in Social Security checks, of which $6,000 could be considered a return for his investment, and another $23,500 in payments over and above the value of what he and his employer had contributed.[5] More embarrassing for everyone is the fact that the richest retired person in America was also receiving that same "welfare" payout of over $23,400 ($165,000 in 2013 dollars). Let's be honest and call it a welfare check, since the recipient was not getting a return from his investment but collecting a no-strings-attached, free "aid in the form of money for those in need." For purposes of definition, let us ignore the fact that some who collected the "welfare" check had no need. They received and accepted the welfare check anyway, as they had never contributed one cent for this "aid in the form of money."[6]

Compare that to his counterpart who had not been so fortunate as to get a job that paid a living wage and therefore paid in less in FICA tax than the maximum. For discussion purposes, let's say he paid in just enough to receive the "subsidized" minimum benefit of $44 per month. In 1967, to qualify for the minimum, a worker had to contribute at least $33 for at least eleven years. The very minimum Mr. Under-paid could have contributed and still qualify for benefits would have been $726, with interest making his contribution worth about $975. No one could possibly have put in only the minimum for just eleven years, so it is unlikely that anyone who qualified for benefits contributed less than $1,000. Since Mr. Under-paid received $528 per year, he used up his contributions in less than three years and began to receive "free" "welfare" money of $528 per year for as long as he lived.

Even though Mr. Under-paid's life expectancy was lower than that of his better-paid counterparts, let's overcompensate and say both lived out the full 14.6 years of the life expectancy of a sixty-five-year-old in 1965. In 14.6 years, Mr. Under-paid received $7,700. To put it bluntly, the "moocher" got back, in under three years, 100 percent of his entire contribution and received 7.7 times his investment, while poor Mr. Better-paid had to wait over three years before collecting his welfare check, and over his lifetime received only 4.9 times his investment, plus interest. There they go again, favoring the poor over the better-off. This "unfair" favoring of the poorest Americans so irked some that in 1981, Congress passed a law to begin *fading out* the minimum "subsidized" benefit. So now a recipient can theoretically receive a monthly payment as low as $1.00.

It is time to look at the facts, not the fantasy story the affluent like to turn into myth. You have seen that the poorest Americans, if they managed to live as long as the affluent—on average they did not—received welfare payments (money over and above what their contributions were worth) of $6,300, while Mr. Better-paid and Mr. Best-paid received welfare payments of $23,400. Where I live, that means Mr. Better-paid received $17,100 more in welfare checks than those living in poverty.[7] To point out the obvious, Mr. Better-paid received a larger welfare check than his neighbor living below the poverty line and struggling to pay for food.

By 1970 both were taking 100 percent of my hard-earned contributions, as they had exhausted their own contributions. So the question that needs to be asked is not whether one received 7.7 times and the other only 2.3 more than his contribution; as demonstrated, both had exhausted their contributions and were relying on current payees to fund 100 percent of their Social Security check, so what they had contributed was irrelevant. The question that needs to be raised and answered is, "How much of current taxpayers' contributions were they taking?"

In 1970 I was working as a college professor and paid in the maximum FICA tax of $655.20 for the year. My contribution covered fifteen months of payments to Mr. Under-paid American but only four months of the subsidy given to the wealthiest retired living American. In other words, the FICA tax I paid into the system covered the welfare payments made to 1.4 of the poorest recipients, while it took the payments of three or more people paying in the maximum to cover the welfare check for the richest American. Clearly you can see that the better-off, including the very richest person in America, was receiving almost four times more of my contribution than the poorest citizen received. Since the affluent lived more than four years longer than the poor, they in fact received an additional $8,000 in 1967 dollars ($56,000 in 2013 money).

Some of the richest (and fewer of the poorest) Americans lived to be one hundred years old. By that time, the wealthiest man had received over $70,500 (of which $64,000 was in welfare payments—that's close to a half a million dollars in today's money), while my less-lucky neighbor would have received about $18,500, an inequity of over $50,000 ($350,000 in 2013 money). To put it another way, the wealthiest American alive who turned one hundred in 2002 had collected in welfare checks the entire FICA payments of four people who were paying in the maximum for thirty-three years. A more pertinent question is, "How many workers paying in the minimum to qualify for benefits did it take to provide 'welfare' benefits to the wealthiest man on the dole?" The answer: more than one hundred. Yes, Mr. Richest Centenarian American in 2002 was collecting the FICA contributions made each and every month for thirty-three years by one hundred citizens living in poverty. Fair? Immoral? Downright disgusting? Extortion? Criminal?

Certainly, you see that there is a huge inequity built into the payout system that overwhelmingly favors the well-off over the poorer recipient. But that is not the worst. What about the workers who paid in for less than ten years—maybe even at the maximum rate? They got nothing. Fair? What about the lowest-paid workers who retired in 1987 and had paid in just below the minimum for forty-one of the fifty years they worked, whose contributions could have grown to be worth over $30,000?[8] Their payout could be zero dollars per month for the rest of their life. Oh, to be so lucky to be poor in America, where the *mythological* government makes laws to redistribute income to the poor, but the *real* government extracts from the poor to augment the wealthy.

You might ask, "If this inequity was true in 1967, 1980 and 1987, is it still true?" The flaw is truer today, for there is no longer a guaranteed minimum, resulting in the poorest being punished more severely. In 1967 the maximum benefit check was 3.8 times the minimum allowed by law. Today the maximum benefit is 5.9 times the representative minimum;[9] but it is possible for the minimum to be even much less. True, Ms. or Mr. Well-paid won't be getting back "free" money quite so quickly. Let's say our worker paid in the maximum for the thirty-five years that are tabulated for payouts. From 1978 through 2012, she and her employer will have paid in about \$270,000. At 3 percent compounded interest, that would be worth about \$390,000.[10] At \$30,400[11] benefits paid per year, that will last about thirteen years—maybe up to fourteen years if interest outperforms inflation.[12] What's a woman's remaining life expectancy at sixty-six? More than nineteen years. Half of all females will live longer. And the affluent have a life expectancy over five years more than those living in poverty. That means more than one-half the Ms. Well-paid citizens will receive more than eight years of free benefits.[13] It will take the payroll tax of eighteen American workers (nine workers if you include the employer's contribution) earning the median salary of \$27,915[14] to pay one retiree, who may be making well over thirteen million dollars per year.[15] Fair, or untenable? Today, the lowest possible Social Security paid to Ms. Under-paid is \$1.00 per month. At that rate, the payments contributed by a worker making the median income will cover the benefits for over 3,400 recipients, while it covers less than six weeks of payments to the richest man in America who is collecting benefits.[16] Fair, shameful, immoral, or unthinkable? Can anyone really believe it is the "damn poor" who are mooching off our society?

To be fair, the minimum for a worker who qualified for Social Security and retired in 2013 is \$431.60, or \$5,179 a year. It changes nothing. Once the retirees run out of their so-called "investment," the equivalent of less than three average workers' Social Security taxes will fund Mr. Under-paid's, while it will take nineteen workers to fund Mr. Well-paid's, including a few billionaires' welfare checks. It would be negligent of me not to mention that this means that all who paid in but did not meet the minimum requirements will get nothing in return for their investment. Yet, upon retiring in 2013, the value of their contribution could be worth over $64,000. Read that again. It is possible for an American citizen, living in poverty for most of his or her life, to have paid enough FICA taxes to be worth $64,000 and receive not one red cent in benefit payments. This tax was collected from America's poorest and was, is, and will be used to subsidize the lifestyle of the richest. My countrymen, what are you thinking?

We have established that the rich reap the most; now let's look at who contributes the most. The poorer citizens pay full tax on 100 percent of their wages, and often that is the only income they have. The wealthy pay only on the first $113,700[17] of their wages and pay nothing on the rest of their income, which is likely to be substantial. A forty-hour-per-week worker making minimum wage of $7.25 per hour earns $15,080 per year and pays $1,869.92 in Social Security tax[18]. To repeat, that is 12.4 percent of the worker's salary (see footnote xvii), and since that worker is unlikely to have other income, it is almost always 12.4 percent of this citizen's *total* income. A citizen making eleven million dollars per year *at most* pays in $14,098.80, or about one-thirteenth of 1 percent of his or her income.[19] Read that again: that is *one-thirteenth of 1 percent*. Yes, the taxpayer making $11 million pays 13 cents for every $100 of *adjusted* gross income, while you pay $12.40 for every $100 of *before-adjusted* gross income. The 14,000 households that make more than eleven million dollars per annum pay in even less. If a person earning $50,000 paid at that rate, they would pay in $65 per year. The minimum-wage worker pays over 124 times what the wealthiest pays.[20] Fair? Or is this one more example of the "damn poor" taking advantage of the system?

It is also true that reserves have grown in recent years. By 2004, what workers were paying in would go out to pay recipients in 2007 and 2008. At the end of 2009, the reserves in the fund had grown to 2.54 trillion dollars, and the payout to recipients was $685.8 billion, meaning there was a 3.7-year surplus. In other words, the money taken in from payroll taxes in 2009 is being used to pay recipients in 2013 and 2014.[21] Unless you began to collect Social Security before September 2014, you will never see one cent of the taxes you paid in any year prior to 2010. Instead, you will be collecting payments from the contributions of *future* generations, just as *you* paid for past generations' benefits. For those who do not need this support, do you really want to take the payments of two American workers who pay in the maximum (have wages of over $113,700), or the FICA taxes of twenty-one workers who have incomes of $12,000 (or, forty-two workers who make $6,000)?[22] If that is you, how do you sleep at night; how can you look in the mirror? Aren't these recipients the true "welfare mamas" that politicians love to rail about?

Since it is unlikely that today's Congress would ever pass a law putting a cap on those who receive benefits, we need to at least make a cap easy to choose for those who do not need the benefits—for those who don't want to look in the mirror to see a person with excess wealth who is taking 100 percent of the FICA payments contributed by forty-two workers who must live on less than $6,000 a year. Can we at least pass a law that states that any person who is legally eligible for Social Security benefits, and whose income puts him or her in the top 5 percent of Americans, does not automatically qualify for benefits? Instead, they must first *opt in* to receive benefits by signing a disclosure statement that says, "I wish to receive my benefits, and I am aware that it will take the contributions of more than forty-two workers who live in poverty to cover my benefit."[23]

Let us think about the fact that *only wages* are taxed for FICA. There is no FICA tax on any other form of income. In other words, workers are being *penalized for working* while other income gets off literally scot-free. Think about it; there are four ways to receive income: from work, investment, a gift, or inheritance. The FICA tax was and is designed to punish one for working, while rewarding those who are given money they did not earn (as a gift or inheritance) or gained from their investments. Fair? Immoral? Fraud?

We have clearly demonstrated that today's recipients are being funded by today's workers, that the rich pay next to nothing, and that the poorest receive by far the least return, if any at all. Is this the kind of program we want to perpetuate into the future?

I make a simple, levelheaded proposal—to go beyond a "patch"—to resolve the Social Security crisis. To both assure future generations of more equitable payout of Social Security and to reset the current scheme, I propose that we establish an individual Secure All Voters Equitably (SAVE) tax-free trust fund for every child born in America from this moment forward. The objective of the account will be to provide each and every newborn American a reasonable assurance that they can move into the retirement years with a guaranteed income at least 150 percent above the poverty line. For children born in 2013, the amount projected for their base social security needs at retirement in 2079—based on projected inflation—will be about $130,000 per year.[24]

The goal will be to invest enough money in each individual's SAVE annuity to provide reasonable assurance that the value of the annuity at age sixty-five can pay $130,000 plus inflation for life, meaning the individual accounts should average about two million dollars. With an expected annual return of 8 percent per year over sixty-six years,[25] each account would need an opening balance of $15,000. In other words, we could fund this part of the proposal for a mere $60 billion per year.[26] The interest that we paid in 2012 for the federal debt was $223 billion.[27] If we can afford that for past mistakes, can't we afford 26.9 percent of that to assure ourselves and our offspring of a bare-bones existence at retirement? We are saddling each and every one of our children with a debt of around $55,000. Couldn't we at least provide them a $15,000 SAVE account? The fund must be set up as an irrevocable trust and operated by the federal government, which our constitution set up to reflect the will and welfare of all the people.

If we kept everything else the same and only added this program, it could be paid for with a FICA tax of 2.33 percent of the total income of the top 1 percent of earners in America, or with a tax of less than 1 percent on the top 10 percent of earners (well below what you and I are paying). This would not require much giveback, considering the enormous benefits they have received from being citizens of the United States of America. As you will soon see, this is not the best solution, but it is one that would be far more equitable and reasonable than what we currently have in place.

Before we get into how America can pay for this investment in the future, let's ask the question: "Do we want to wait sixty-six more years to completely resolve the problems created over the past seventy-six years?" Even if we wanted to take sixty-six years to address the inequity, we cannot, as experts project that the current system will only be able to cover about 75 percent of the demands made on it in thirty-three years. In other words, we will need to supplement the income of retirees who are currently in their mid-thirties or younger who will begin retiring on or about 2046. If we are going to expect this group of individuals to continue to supply payroll tax to cover Americans now over thirty-three, we will need to assure them they will be able to receive a fair retirement benefit relative to those retiring both before and after they do.

Therefore, I propose that we cover this gap by creating a group SAVE annuity to cover each citizen turning thirty-three for the next thirty-two years in order to assure every citizen a minimum retirement benefit at age sixty-six. For those turning thirty-three, we need only provide 25 percent (more for the impoverished citizen) of their need, with the rest coming from maintaining the current system.[28] The math here is more complicated, but it will take setting aside about $52 billion a year for this account.[29]

How are we are going to pay for the two SAVE funds and keep the current system afloat? You guessed it: we need to revise the way FICA is determined and provide a simple way for those who *do not* need benefits to reinvest them for the future of our citizenry. Step one is to stop penalizing those who earn money and start charging unearned income (gifts and inheritance) and investment income at least the same as income from labor.[30] The need to maintain the current system and add the individual SAVE account for all newborn children, and the group SAVE annuity for all citizens on their thirty-third birthday, is about $950 billion per annum. The total personal income of all Americans is estimated at $13.4 trillion. If each person paid in what the poorest citizens currently pay (12.5 percent of their total income), that would create a revenue pool of over $1.67 trillion, almost $700 billion more than required. By distributing the responsibility to pay for Social Security equally, we could lower the FICA rate from 12.4 percent to 7 percent, while adding both SAVE accounts. Still, that would not be the most equitable solution. A fairer approach would be to require all households in the top two quintiles to pay 8 percent FICA tax. This is 4.2 percent less than some are paying now. For wage earners, the employee and the employer would each pay 4 percent. Income from investments, inheritance, and gifts would be treated as self-employed income, and the recipient would pay the entire amount due, as is now the case for those that are self-employed. Those taxpaying units with income in the bottom three quintiles would pay a declining percentage, with those below two times the poverty line paying 1 percent, to be matched by their employer.[31] The formula for that rate reduction is beyond the scope of this paper but could easily be computed by the Treasury or Social Security departments. Every citizen with an income would be paying between 2 percent and 8 percent FICA tax—a nice reduction from the current 12.4 percent.[32]

Nearly all Americans see advantages in the government keeping and managing the Social Security trust, and many see the advantages of each citizen having an individual account. So far, we have not conceived a way to do that—in part because the Republicans demand we turn the current system into unsupervised individual investment accounts, and the Democrats insist the government maintain 100 percent control. We can have our cake and eat it too. My proposal for the future generations relies on group-managed individual accounts and for those under thirty-three a *mix* of a group annuity account and the present system. The current system must stay as it is, except for tweaking it to rebalance the inequities granted on behalf of the rich.

There is no need to reinvent the mechanism of operating the SAVE trust. To meet the objective of providing reasonable assurance of each individual receiving a minimum of $130,000 annually from Social Security in the year 2079, we can establish an annuity fund based on the successful model established by TIAA-CREF (the Teachers Insurance and Annuity Association of America–College Retirement Equities Fund) that was in force until about 1990. In that system, each individual owns his or her account, has limited flexibility on how the funds can be invested, and has the option of turning all investments at the time of retirement into an annuity that guarantees payments of 6.5 percent of the value of the annuity at time of retirement, if the investor takes no guaranteed number of years for spouse or offspring.[33] Since every American will be invested in this plan from birth, with current taxpayers' dollars, there will be no need or reason to pass on the investment to spouse or offspring. Any balance other than a one-time grant for burial left in an account at a person's death will roll back into the overall value of the annuity fund, thus assuring a return of 6.5 percent for the living retirees.[34]

We have left some problems unresolved. To solve Medicare may take more ingenuity. This platform does not address Social Security benefits for the disabled. It seems reasonable to conclude that the current system can continue to successfully address their need. Nor does it resolve the need for immigrants to be covered by Social Security. Solutions to these needs can be resolved after we debate and put into place a SAVE trust for every newborn American and a group annuity for those born thirty-three years ago.

Persons more familiar with the way to write a law than I am will need to address a way to prohibit future legislatures or the court from dissolving these individual accounts. Also, they must address the fact that those funded "up front" may not want to pay FICA tax to cover the retirement years of those who paid to establish their trust fund. There must be a way to prevent that. One possible way would require that the SAVE accounts be used to pay for current retirees if and when Congress or the people decide to stop paying in to cover the benefits of retirees at any time over the next sixty-six years. If that happens, the individual trust funds need to be collapsed into the overall fund to take care of the current retirees. That should discourage any tampering with the plan.

Note that once this plan is in place, the total cost to taxpayers will be significantly reduced in thirty-three years, and in sixty-six years the cost will be reduced to the equivalent of $700 per taxpayer per year, obviously some paying more and others less. Nice replacement of the current $1,800 paid by one on minimum wage, the $3,461 now paid by the median income earner, and the $14,600 paid by those whose salaries are $117,000 or more. More importantly, the benefits will be more evenly distributed. As Chaucer might have said, "Cheap, at ten percent the price."[35]

I have offered a long-range plan to resolve over the next thirty-three years (see footnote xxviii for a twenty-two-year plan) most of the problems existing from a program that was built on false promises and legalized inequity. The solution is a no-brainer, offering a more equitable system, assuring a sounder future, requiring only a little tweaking, and a reduction in FICA rates for all. As William Carlos Williams said about another situation:

> Or do you think you can shut greed in? [36]
> What—from us? We who have perhaps
> nothing to lose? Share with us
> share with us—it will be money
> in your pockets.
> Go now
> I think you are ready.

BOOK I

TIME TO JOURNEY HOME

Appendices

James & Marlys Venner

APPENDIX A

Ahnentafel Story

Identified prior to April 17, 2009

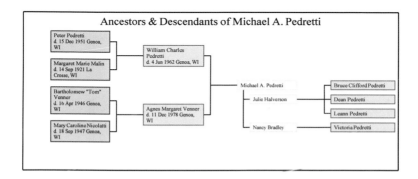

The following story was compiled by James Venner and given to the author in the spring of 2009; this is a reprint of Jim's data file. It is the ahnentafel story of the Pedretti-Venner family—in this case tracing the ancestry of the author back to Antonio Buzzetti, born in 1569 in Vhò, a village just south of Campodolcino. Those who are participating in chronicling our family have since identified more than four hundred additional ancestors, but this list represents where we were as I began my journey described in this book. I did take the liberty to add some information I thought the reader would want to know; the information that was added to Venner's original documentation is enclosed in parentheses ( ).

In order to present the information about our family as accurately as possible, I have inserted inside brackets [ ] information gained through research since 2009 that replaces older theories. For example, "Mary Caroline NICOLATTI born 20 Feb 1880 in Trieste [Trento], Austria" shows that in 2009 we thought Mary Caroline was born in Trieste, but new documentation proves she was born in Trento.

Later volumes of *The Story of Our Stories* will include all known ancestors of the main character at the time of printing.

Generation 1

1. Michael[1] PEDRETTI, born 17 April 1942 in La Crosse, Wisconsin, son of 2 William Charles Pedretti and 3 Agnes Margaret Venner.

Michael Arthur Pedretti comes from a large family. His grandparents Pedretti had eleven children and 74 grandchildren; his grandparents Venner had 9 children and 52 grandchildren. Since four Pedrettis married four Venners and his parents had 15 children, Mike only has 86 first cousins, of which 24 are double first cousins. His parents, William and Agnes Pedretti, had 13 children and 71 grandchildren. The number of children and grandchildren given are those that survived infancy. Children who were stillborn or died shortly after birth have not been included.

Michael was raised in Genoa, Wisconsin, as were both of his parents and two of his grandparents (Peter Pedretti and Bartholomew "Tom" Venner). His grandma Pedretti was born in Sharpsburg, PA, a suburb of Pittsburgh, and his grandma Venner was born in Trento, Italy—it was part of Austria when she was born. His most removed ancestor to immigrate to America was his great-great-great-grandmother, Mary Ann Buzzetti Zaboglio, who immigrated with her son shortly after her daughter, son-in-law, and granddaughter (Mike's great-grandmother) arrived in Genoa in 1852. All were born in Campodolcino, Sondria, Lombardy, Italy.

All of his ancestors immigrated to America in the twenty-nine years between 1852 and 1881 on or near the times recorded in the chart at the end of the appendices to this book.

His ancestors came from Italy, Austria, Bohemia (now the Czech Republic), and Switzerland. It is almost certain that 12 of his 16 great-great-grandparents were Italians (Pedretti, Cerletti, Lombardi, Formi, Vener, Della Morte, Sterlocchi, Zaboglio, Nichelati, Chiogna, Gabrielli, and Fruet). While there were a variety of reasons they immigrated, it can be noted that Italians from the region of Mike's ancestors most often immigrated to avoid being conscripted into the Prussian army to fight foreign wars. The Prussians liked to conscript Italians because of their reputations as fierce fighters and of course because they were not the sons of Austrian or German mothers.

Two of Mike's great-great-grandparents were born in Austria and were probably Austrian (Malin and Erne), and two were born in Bohemia (Guentner—believed to be Bohemian—and Krause, whose parents were from Germany). This would make Mike 12.5 percent Austrian, and 12.5 percent German-Bohemian-Czech. With the name Guentner and Krause and the part of Bohemia they came from considered German-Bohemia, it may be safe to conclude there is a mixture of Bohemian and German or Czech blood in that 12.5 percent. Of course Mike would prefer to think that Albert Guentner was Bohemian and not

German. His mother often told him that he was one-eighth Bohemian; he hopes she was correct.

Michael worked as a farmer, a baker, and a bartender and held many part-time jobs, taught in college, produced international theater festivals, renovated a few abandoned houses, and writes essays, fiction, and poetry as well as historical works such as *The Story of Our Stories.*

Generation 2

2. William[2] PEDRETTI, born 6 Jan 1900 in Genoa, Vernon, Wisconsin; died 4 Jun 1962 in Genoa, Vernon, Wisconsin; buried in St. Charles Cemetery, Genoa, Wisconsin, son of 4. Peter PEDRETTI and 5. Margaret Marie MALIN. He married on 15 Nov 1922 in Genoa, Vernon, Wisconsin.

3. Agnes M. VENNER, born 12 Apr 1903 in Genoa, Vernon, Wisconsin; died 11 Dec 1978 in Genoa, Vernon, Wisconsin; buried in St. Charles Cemetery, Genoa, Wisconsin, daughter of 6. Bartholomew "Tom" VENNER and 7. Mary Caroline NICOLATTI.

William Pedretti and Agnes Venner
Wedding
Best Man Peter Pedretti; Maid of Honor Mae Venner
November 15, 1922

Notes for William PEDRETTI

William Charles Pedretti operated a farm in Genoa, Wisconsin. He was born in his grandma Pedretti's log cabin, on January 6, 1900, to Peter Pedretti and Margaret Malin Pedretti, the third in a family of 11 children. When he was 8, his family moved to the Mound Ridge farm, which William later purchased. He attended the Mound Ridge School, which was located on the SE corner of this farm, to grade 5, and was self-educated after that. He served on the Board of Education of Mound Ridge Elementary School for several years. He liked to read and was interested in learning and passed on his love of books to his family. Bill attended the St. Charles Church so probably met his future bride Agnes Venner there. His father's farm touched kitty corner with Agnes' parents' farm, so it seems likely they, from time to time, snuck off to the woods separating the farms.

Bill's mother passed away on September 14, 1921. One year and one day later Bill married Agnes Margaret Venner, oldest child of Bartholomew Venner and Mary Nickelatti. Agnes and Bill lived with his father's family for a short time after their marriage. Bill and Agnes purchased the Mound Ridge farm from his father on May 20, 1924. Bill often stated with pride that even in the depths of the depression he never missed a farm payment to his father. They lived there until February 1949, when their house burned down.

Bill had an accordion and could play "Home, Sweet Home" on it. He enjoyed hunting and fishing and attending free outdoor movies in the summer with the children. He also took his entire family to the County Fair in Viroqua in the summertime. He was an innovative farmer adapting strip farming early on. For several years he traveled with his trophy jackass to service area horses and donkeys when in heat. He was a gifted mechanic and always took care of the Hart Parr and kept the machinery running during thrashing, and was known to give his best friend, Frank Jambois, a hand at his gas station garage. Bill was an avid hunter and fisherman. He took great pride in his hunting dogs, and his dog Queenie placed fourth in 1952 Western Wisconsin Fox and Coon hunting bench show. This was especially impressive as Queenie was not a verifiable purebred and Bill had no previous experience in showing a dog in a competitive show.

Farm work was done with a team of horses until Bill got a tractor in the 1940s. There was no electricity in the home until 1935. They did have running cold water, which Bill had piped in from the windmill on the hill above the house. It came in by gravity. He also put in an indoor toilet and a tub that had only cold running water, so water had to be heated on the range to add to the cold water. Before the tub was put in, baths were taken in a galvanized tub in front of the oven in the kitchen. This happened once a week, on Saturday nights.

After the Mound Ridge farmhouse burned to the ground, Bill and Agnes moved their family to the house where Agnes grew up. Luckily, Bill and Agnes had purchased the farm and home the year before, shortly after Agnes's parents passed away. Bill and Agnes lived there until 1956, when they retired to the former Monti home in the village of Genoa. In 1964 Bill became ill and passed away shortly after enduring colon surgery

Agnes[2] Venner was the first born of Bartholomew "Tom" Venner, who was the fourth child of Giovanni Venner and Mary Starlochi. Her mother, Mary Caroline Nicolatti, gave birth to Agnes on April 12, 1903, in their freshly built house on the farm that Tom had recently purchased from his father's estate. She was from a family of ten children, namely Mae, Helen, Bert, Francis, Greg, Johnny, Philip, Rita, and Charles. Charles died the same day he was born.

Agnes attended St. Charles Catholic School for 9 years, taking grade 8 for two years because she enjoyed school so much. She worked as a teacher assistant at St. Charles. Agnes and Bill had 15 children, the first in 1924 and the last in 1946, so they were kept busy. Their first two, Agnes and Anna, were born at St. Ann's Hospital in La Crosse. Clara, Bernard, Dolores, Joseph, Margaret, Bill, Joan, and Mary Jane were born at home. After that, Daniel, Mike, twin boys, James and John, who died shortly after birth, and the last, Leo, were all born in St. Ann's hospital in La Crosse, Wisconsin. Agnes was pregnant 126 months—over 45 percent of the 23 years from the time she conceived Agnes and gave birth to Leo (circa 23 July 1923 to 1 July 1946).

Agnes and Bill had a large brick home on the farm and raised grain, corn, and hay for the animals, and Agnes had a large garden of vegetables. There was a potato patch, strawberry, blackberry, and raspberry patches, grape vines, apple and plum trees, plus cows, pigs, and chickens to provide food for the family. It was a little Garden of Eden, but there was always lots of work to do: milk cows, hoe and harvest corn, make hay, and pitch hay from the barn loft in the winter and silage from the silo to keep the cows and horses fed. The house had six bedrooms, so the family was not crowded. There was a cool dirt basement with a root cellar for keeping food.

Agnes was always busy with a baby, housework, and church activities. She had no time for recreation. She did enjoy visiting their parents and brothers' and sisters' families, who all lived on farms close by, and reunion picnics were held almost every summer.

The school was just up the hill from the farmhouse so it was handy for the children to attend. The children also attended catechism on Saturdays and for two weeks during the summertime. The church held an annual picnic on July 4th every year, which everyone enjoyed. Agnes prepared chicken, risot (the local name for risotto), and pies for the dinner. After meals were served, she loved to play bingo. She raised a large garden of vegetables and flowers throughout her retirement and often gave her children canned corn, peas, and bags of saffron. She died alone at home on December 11, 1978.

Generation 3

4. Peter[3] PEDRETTI, born 25 Jan 1861 [before Lincoln was inaugurated] in Genoa, Vernon, Wisconsin; died 15 Dec 1951 in Genoa, Vernon, Wisconsin; buried in St. Charles Cemetery, Genoa, Wisconsin, son of 8. Stephen PEDRETTI and 9. Adelaide LOMBARDI. He married on 26 Nov 1895 in Genoa, Vernon, Wisconsin.

5. Margaret Marie MALIN, born 11 Jun 1876 in Sharpsburg, Allegheny, PA; died 14 Sep 1921 in La Crosse, Wisconsin; buried in St. Charles Cemetery, Genoa, Wisconsin, daughter of 10. F. Joseph MALIN and 11. Margaret Marie GUENTNER.

Notes for Peter PEDRETTI
(Peter's story will be told in detail in Book 8 of this series.)

Notes for Margaret Marie MALIN
 Death: Death Certificate, Vernon County, Wisconsin, Volume 11, page 475. She died of a blood disorder.
 Sharpsburg, PA, is a suburb of Pittsburgh. Margaret was called Maggie by the Malin family.

6. Bartholomew "Tom"[3] VENNER, born 17 Nov 1873 in Genoa, Vernon, Wisconsin; died 16 Apr 1946 in Genoa, Vernon, Wisconsin; buried in St. Charles Cemetery, Genoa, Wisconsin, son of 12. John Baptist "Giovanni" VENNER and 13. Mary Madelina "Maria Maddalena" STARLOCHI. He married on 29 Apr 1902 in Genoa, Vernon, Wisconsin.

7. Mary Caroline NICOLATTI, born 20 Feb 1880 in Trieste, Austria (Trento, Italy); died 18 Sep 1947 in Genoa, Vernon, Wisconsin; buried in St. Charles Cemetery, Genoa, Wisconsin, daughter of 14. John M. NICHELATTI and 15. Margaret GABRIEL.

Four Generations

Mary Nicolatti-Venner with daughter, Agnes Venner-
Pedretti; great-granddaughter Mary Agnes Dahl; and
granddaughter, Agnes Pedretti-Dahl
1946

Nine of Agnes' first eleven children posing before the
Mound Ridge farmhouse, 1940
Back row: Agnes, Daniel, Clara, Ann
Front Row: Dolores, Margaret, Joan, William
Sitting: Mary Jane
Not in Photo - Bernard & Joseph

1895

Peter Pedretti and Maggie Malin wedding, November
26, 1895

Grandpa Peter Pedretti + grandchildren 1941

Clara,Carol,Carl,Alvin,Agnes,Ray,Bernard,Lawrence

Mary Lee Stowe held by Marie,Ann,Pat held by Frank,Lucy, Marvin,Dolores,Don,Shirley Levi,Terese,Arni

Ron,Ralph,Geraldine Levi,Joan,Marge,Jim P.,Jim V., Joe, Bill,Rita,Marilyn

(to the right of Grandpa Pete): Bob,Donna Levi,Duane,Ken, Berneal

Tom V.,Ed,Dan,Mary Jane,Dorothy

This photograph was taken at the family's celebration of Peter Pedretti's 80th birthday. He is seen here with 43 of his grandchildren. If name listed is just a first name, the person's last name is Pedretti. Peter had 30 more grandchildren after this photograph was taken.

Another photograph of Peter with grandchildren,

The family celebrated Peter's birthday during the summer after he turned 80 on January 25, 1941. Peter was born a few months before Abraham Lincoln was sworn in as the sixteenth President of the United States.

Back Row Clara, Carol, Carl, Alvin, Agnes, Ray,
Bernard, and Lawrence
Third Row: Mary Lee Stowe held by Marie, Ann, Pat
held by Frank, Lucy, Marvin, Dolores, Don, Shirley
Levi, Teresa, and Arni
Second Row: Ron, Ralph, Geraldine Levi, Joan, Margaret,
Jim, Jim Venner, Joe, Bill, Rita, Marilyn, Grandpa Peter,
Bob, Donna Levi, Duane Venner, Ken, and Berneal
Sitting: Tom Venner, Ed, Dan, Mary Jane, and Dorothy
Note: If only first name given, the last name is Pedretti

Tom Venner (1873-1946).

Notes for Bartholomew "Tom" VENNER

Death: Death Certificate, Vernon County, Wisconsin, Volume 22, page 106.

He went by the name of Tom. In 1900 Tom worked in Cumberland Wisconsin area working in forestry. After his parents died he took over the original John Venner farm east of Genoa, Wisconsin, and married Mary Nicolatti. As a matter of interest, four children of Tom and Mary Venner's family married four children from the adjoining farm of Peter and Margaret Pedretti.

Notes for Mary Caroline[3] NICOLATTI

Death: Death Certificate, Vernon County, Wisconsin, Volume 22, page 507.

Mary came to the US in 1881 per 1900 census. Also, she often said that she came to the US when she was 1 year old. She always had her garden, where she raised much of her family's food. Just before her death she donated to St. Charles Church a stained glass window with a picture of the Blessed Virgin that is located over the main alter. (There is some evidence she had not completed the gift prior to her death and her daughters secretly provided cash found in Mary's house to compete the gift.) The window is presently covered over in a remodeling activity. (Window is now on display suspended above the altar.)

Generation 4

8. Stephen[4] PEDRETTI, born 15 Aug 1826 in San Bernardo, Sondrio, Italy; died 1 Apr 1869 in Genoa,

Vernon, Wisconsin; buried in St. Charles Cemetery, Genoa, Wisconsin, son of 16. Guglielmo "William" PEDRETTI and 17. Teresa CERLETTI. He married on 6 Feb 1858 in Harmony, Bad Ax, Wisconsin

9. Adelaide LOMBARDI, born 28 Jul 1830 in Locarno (Airolo), Ticino, Switzerland; died 10 Feb 1911 in Genoa, Vernon, Wisconsin; buried 13 Feb 1911 in St. Charles Cemetery, Genoa, Wisconsin, daughter of 18. Peter LOMBARDI and 19. Magdalene FORMI (Forni).

Notes for Stephen PEDRETTI

Stephen with his brothers Wilhelm (William) and Sylvester came to the US on the ship Connecticut from Havre (Le Havre, France); arrived in New York on 23 August 1854. Stephen and Sylvester went on to Genoa. William went to California. (He relocated to California after settling in Genoa.)

The brothers came from San Bernardo, Sondrio, Italy. Stephen settled on a farm just east of Genoa on section No. 27 in Genoa Township, Vernon County, Wisconsin. Stephen is buried in St. Charles Cemetery in Genoa, and on his tombstone it states: "A Native of St. Bernard, Italy, He Left a Wife and Five Children." His brother Sylvester helped the family after Stephen was crushed and killed by a timber as he was erecting a barn.

Stephen's marriage license was issued in Harmony Township, Bad Ax County (Vernon) on Feb. 6, 1858. This was found by Jean Pedretti Flottmeyer.

Marriage certificate: Vernon County, Wisconsin, Volume B, page 18. Birth and death dates from observation of markings on grave marker in Genoa, Wisconsin. 1 Apr 1869 as date he died from being crushed by a timber while building a barn and date of birth calculated as marker says he was 43 years old. (Birth data has since been verified by records help in San Bernardo church in Italy.)

Notes for Adelaide[4] LOMBARDI
Birth/Death Dates: From death certificate, Volume 7, page 610, Vernon County Wisconsin.

After she became a widow with 5 children, Adelaide went to San Bernardino, California, area to live near a brother-in-law, William Pedretti. Later the family came back to Wisconsin. Also, her daughter Madeline was born with serious respiratory problems and the family hoped that sunny California would benefit her. Adelaide came from Switzerland in 1856 per the 1900 Genoa, Wisconsin, census records.

10. F. Joseph[4] MALIN, born 16 Aug 1847 in Gofis, Austria; died 7 May 1898 in Genoa, Vernon, Wisconsin; buried in St. Charles Cemetery, Genoa, Wisconsin, son of 20. Josef Anton MALIN and 21. Anne Marie ERNE. He married on 31 Aug 1875 in St. Mary Parish, Sharpsburg, Allegheny, PA.

11. Margaret Marie GUENTNER, born 5 Jan 1853 in Egere [Petlarn], Bohemia; died 12 Apr 1926 in Genoa, Vernon, Wisconsin; buried in St. Charles Cemetery, Genoa,

Wisconsin, daughter of 22. Albert GUENTNER and 23. Elizabeth KRAUSE.

Notes for F. Joseph MALIN

F. Joseph Malin with three brothers John, Alois, and Paul came to America in 1872. The "F" in his name stood for Franz. The brothers were born in Gofis near Feldkirch, Austria. They lived in Pennsylvania until 1876 when they moved to Wisconsin. Alois, John, and Joseph settled in La Crosse. F. Joseph farmed just east of Genoa. F. Joseph had worked in a blast furnace in Pennsylvania. A hot cinder had got into one of his eyes and destroyed its sight. The eye was never removed. In the words of his wife, Margaret, "Papa's lungs were poor and he had to suffer much. I don't know how often he had pneumonia. His last sickness was inflammation of the bowels. There wasn't anything the doctors could do." Margaret rose in the dead of night and, scared stiff, walked to Genoa to get the priest for Extreme Unction. The priest stayed until morning. The wolves howled around the house all night.

The Malins knew the Brendels, Brittings, and Rohrers, Germans who came to Genoa one year earlier than the Malins had.

Marriage/Birth: Certificate from St. Mary Church, Sharpsburg, provides date of marriage for F. Joseph and Margaret Guentner and birth dates for Margaret and Paul. St. Mary is at 210 Pennsylvania Street, Pittsburg, PA 15215.

Birth/Death: Dates from St. Charles Cemetery records.

Notes for Margaret Marie[4] GUENTNER

Margaret Marie Guentner was the oldest of the children of Albert and Elizabeth Guentner. She immigrated to America in 1873, the first of her family to do so. Her passport, issued in Austria, is dated May 3, 1870. She lived in the German settlement of Sharpsburg, PA, a suburb of Pittsburgh, PA, where she worked as a hired girl. Margaret was afraid that she would get sick and have no one to take care of her. After expressing a desire to return to Bohemia, she was asked to stay with the promise that the family would join her in America.

Birth/Death: Dates from St. Charles burial records.

Death: Death Certificate, Vernon County, Wisconsin, Volume13, page 364.

Standing, top row: Albert, Margaret, Paul, Mary. Second row: Alois, John
Seated (l-r) Elizabeth, Frank, Margaret Guentner Malin, Johanna, F. Joseph Malin, Joseph
Picture was taken in 1897. Not pictured: Theresa (died 1896)

Franz Joseph Malin and Margaret Marie Guentner with their children. I believe the child identified as Frank is actually Theresa and that this picture was taken at Peter and Maggie's wedding. Photo 1895

12. John Baptist "Giovanni"[4] VENNER, born 13 Mar 1829 in Campodolcino, Sondrio, Italy; died 13 Mar 1900 in Viroqua, Vernon, Wisconsin; buried in St. Charles Cemetery, Genoa, Wisconsin, son of 24. Giovanni Battista VENER and 25. Margarita DELLA MORTE. He married about 1867 in Genoa, Vernon, Wisconsin.

13. Mary Madelina "Maria Maddalena" STARLOCHI, born 18 Apr 1851 in Campodolcino, Sondrio, Italy; died 10 May 1899 in Genoa, Vernon, Wisconsin; buried in St. Charles Cemetery, Genoa, Wisconsin, daughter of 26. Bartholomew "Bartolomeo" STARLOCHI and 27. Mary Ann "Marianna" ZABOLIO.

Notes for John Baptist "Giovanni" VENNER

Birth date from scroll of the Sterlocchi family received by Rosemarie Marchetti Smith in 1997. Date of death from death certificate No. 25 of Vernon County, Wisconsin, lists his birth date as 1830. I believe the scroll date is more accurate.

John Venner came to America in 1856 from the Campodolcino, Sondrio, Italy. The family name Vener comes from around Prestone, which is near Gallivaggio and is located southeast of Campodolcino. His baptized name in Italy was Giovanni Battista. We have found a record of land being sold by an Antonio Vener, son of Rocco, dated in 1733 in the area.

We believe that John and his brother Frank immigrated through New Orleans around 1856 then traveled by steam boat up the Mississippi to Genoa. [They came over in a ship from Le Havre and landed in New York.] Did they find the bluffs around Genoa to remind them of their familiar homeland and choose it as their home? Or was it the fact that others from their home village area were making their home in Genoa?

The brothers are listed in the Genoa census of 1860. Their father was Giovanni Vener who was married to a Margarita, last name not known (Della Morte). John settled in Genoa Township, Vernon County, Wisconsin, about one mile east of Genoa.

As of today the farm is still owned by a member of the family. Sometime in the late 1800s the John Venner family changed the spelling of their name from Vener to Venner. The family of his brother Frank did not change the spelling of their name from Vener.

The family's life was a hard one, having to clear the forested hillsides, build a cabin and sheds for the animals, all on the frontier, and make it into a farm with little resources other than their own efforts. His wife, while much younger than he, preceded him in death. Like many of the male pioneers he married late and then died, leaving children as orphans to go through a difficult childhood. John himself was in poor health for the last several years of his life.

While John has a death certificate, Vernon County, Wisconsin, Volume 3, page 38, that lists his birth as 1830, I question if the appropriate information was listed. Throughout his life his age is listed as being younger than his brother Frank. Only on his death certificate is he older.

(John's diary is the main story of Book 7 of this series.)

Notes for Mary Madelina[4] "Maria Maddalena" STARLOCHI

Birth: Date from Josephine Ott's Bible. Death: From grave marker at St. Charles Cemetery in Genoa, Wisconsin. Also, birth date from scroll of the Sterlocchi family received by Rosemarie Marchetti Smith in 1997.

14. John M.[4] NICHELATTI, born 6 Apr 1850 in Bolzano, Austria (1851 in Cognola, Trentino); died 17 Aug 1932 in La Crosse, Wisconsin; buried 20 Aug 1932 in St. Charles Cemetery, Genoa, Wisconsin, son of 28. Michael NICHELATTI and 29. (---) ANTONETTE (Maria Antonia Chiogna). He married in 1878 in Austria.

15. Margaret GABRIEL, born 16 Feb 1855 in Trieste, Austria (Levico, Trentino); died 23 Jul 1926 in Genoa, Vernon, Wisconsin; buried 25 Jul 1926 in St. Charles Cemetery, Genoa, Wisconsin, daughter of 30. John GABRIEL and 31. Ursula FANETTI (Orsola Fruet).

Notes for John M. NICHELATTI

Few families use more variations in the spelling of their surname than the Nichelatti family. Versions of the name include Nicolatti and Nickelatti and others. The death certificates of John and Margaret were issued with their surname spelled differently. Reviewing similar names in use today in Italy, the prevalent spelling is Nicoletti, with very few use the spelling Nicolatti. My guess the family descends from the Italian Nicoletti family. (The family came from Trento area where their name was spelled Nichelati.)

The Nichelatti family came to America in 1881. Mary Nicoletti Venner was born in 1880 [and] related that she was one year old when the family came to the USA.

The Nichelattis settled in Norway, MI. Later, about 1883, they settled on a farm east of Genoa now on County Trunk K in Section 22 and 23 of Genoa Township. The date of the first deed recorded to John Nichelatti is 18 July 1883; the deed shows he paid 800 dollars for 20 acres, purchasing the acreage from John Ott. The farm ownership to this day remains in the family. The census records for the year 1900 state they came from Austria. However, with Austrian boundary changes that occurred after World War I, the cities they came from are now part of Italy. He sometimes went by the name of Giovanni Nickelotti. According to the 1900 census records the family was naturalized in 1881 in PA.

Birth/Death Dates from his death certificate filed in Register 416A La Crosse County, Wisconsin.

Notes for Margaret GABRIEL[4]

Margaret was born and raised in Trieste, Austria (later we discovered she was born in Levico, Trentino). She started out studying to become a nun. However, she did not get along with the Mother Superior so she went to work for a rich family in Trento, Austria. That is where she met John.

Margaret Gabriel Nichelatti's brother Joseph Gabriel's wife died in Genoa in 1884 leaving Joseph with no one to care for his three children. Joseph moved from Genoa to the state of Washington to make a living, where he worked in the mining trade. He left his three children with John and Margaret where they grew up with the twelve Nichelatti children. In the 1900 census an Anna Gabriel was identified as a 16-year-old niece still living with the Nick family. The original Nick family home was small and very basic. How 16 children made it in that house is hard to imagine.

Birth/death dates from her death certificate filed in volume 13, page 441, Vernon County, Wisconsin.

Mary Nicolatti-Venner
with her parents Margaret Gabriel and John Nickelatti
Photo circa 1919

Generation 5

16. Guglielmo "William"[5] PEDRETTI, born 17 Apr 1804 in San Bernardo, , Sondrio, Italy; died 1 Dec 1869 in San Bernardo, , Sondrio, Italy. He married about 1824 in San Bernardo, Sondrio, Italy 17. Teresa CERLETTI

Notes for Guglielmo "William" PEDRETTI
Information on birth and death data from Sue Pedretti visit to Italy in August of 1996.

18. Peter[5] LOMBARDI, born in Switzerland; died in Switzerland. He married 19. Magdalene FORMI (FORNI), born in Switzerland.

Notes for Peter LOMBARDI
Names from daughter Adelaide Lombardi Pedretti death certificate. Vernon County Wisconsin. Register number 2.

Notes for Magdalene[5] FORNI
Name from the death certificate of Adelaide Lombardi Pedretti.

Children of Peter LOMBARDI and Magdalene FORNI were as follows:
9I Adelaide[4] LOMBARDI, born 28 Jul 1830 in Locarno, (Airolo) Ticino, Switzerland; died 10 Feb 1911 in Genoa, Vernon, Wisconsin; buried 13 Feb 1911 in St Charles Cemetery, Genoa, Wisconsin. She married on 6 Feb 1858

in Harmony, Badax, Wisconsin Stephen PEDRETTI, born 15 Aug 1826 in San Bernardo, Sondrio, Italy; died 1 Apr 1869 in Genoa, Vernon, Wisconsin; buried in St Charles Cemetery, Genoa, Wisconsin, son of Guglielmo "William" PEDRETTI and Teresa CERLETTI.

20. Josef Anton[5] MALIN, died in Feldkirch, Austria. He married 21. Anne Marie ERNE, born in Austria; died in Feldkirch, Austria.

Notes for Josef Anton MALIN

Josef Anton Malin is assumed to have died in Austria. Josef was a Frenchman. He owned and operated a textile factory (embroidery and insertions) in Feldkirch, Austria.

22. Albert[5] GUENTNER, born 19 May 1816 in Eger, Bohemia; died 16 Aug 1889 in La Crosse, Wisconsin; buried in Catholic Cemetery, La Crosse, Wisconsin. He married 23. Elizabeth KRAUSE, born 21 Jan 1832 in Egere, Bohemia; died 25 Sep 1914 in La Crosse, Wisconsin; buried in Catholic Cemetery, La Crosse, Wisconsin, daughter of 32. Michael KRAUSE.

Notes for Albert GUENTNER

Albert Guentner and his wife Elizabeth with their family came to America from Egere, Bohemia. They settled for a time in Sharpsburg, Pa. and then moved to La Crosse, Wisconsin.

Notes for Elizabeth[5] KRAUSE
Came to the US in 1884

24. Giovanni Battista[5] VENER, born 15 Oct 1793 in Sondrio, Italy; died 8 Sep 1869 in Sondrio, Italy. He married on 1 Apr 1813 in Italy 25. Margarita DELLA MORTE, born 1799 in Sondrio, Italy; died 28 Jul 1842 in Sondrio, Italy.

Notes for Giovanni Battista VENER
Name of father Giovanni and Margherita from Death Certificate of Mary Ann Vener. Todd County, Minn. Number E-106-14.

26. Bartholomew "Bartolomeo"[5] STARLOCHI, born 24 Sep 1825 in Campodolcino, Sondrio, Italy; died 5 Aug 1900 in St. Paul, Ramsey, MN; buried 7 Aug 1900 in Sacred Heart, Aberdeen, Brown, SD, son of 33. Agostino Giuseppe STERLOCCHI and 34. Maddalena GIANOLI. He married on 5 Mar 1847 in St Mary, (Our Lady of Mercy) Gallivaggio, Sondrio, Italy 27. Mary Ann "Marianna" ZABOLIO, born 17 Dec 1823 in Campodolcino, Sondrio, Italy; died 6 Feb 1905 in Aberdeen, Brown, SD; buried 7 Feb 1905 in Sacred Heart, Aberdeen, Brown, SD, daughter of 35. Francesco Giuseppe ZABOGLIO and 36. Maria Teresa Domenica Petronilla BUZZETTI.

Notes for Bartholomew "Bartolomeo" STARLOCHI
Birth/Death: From the Aberdeen Daily News Obituary write up. Also Bartholomew birth and death listed in the Ott's family Bible and birth date from scroll of the

Sterlocchi Family received by Rosemarie Marchetti Smith in 1997. Marriage date and location from Parochial Certificate from Italy.

Many questions exist pertaining to the spelling of the Starlocki family name with conflicting data provided. One is the spelling of the name, at least in the US. I remember a discussion with a cousin over should the name be spelled Starlochi or Starlocki? The grave marker has the name spelled as Starlochi. His obituary spells the name as Starlochi. Bart (under the Homestead Act) was awarded title to land in Spink County. His name is recorded in the paper in the name of Bartholomew Starlocki. Well as it turns out all of the spellings above are not correct; the name in Italy as used by the family is spelled as Sterlocchi.

In this book I use the spelling normally used in the US not the spelling used in Italy.

The following is a copy of the obituary write up of Bart Starlochi as published by "The Aberdeen Daily News" dated Aug. 6, 1900.

Death of B. Starlochi.

Death Ends His suffering in St Paul Sunday Forenoon

A telegram received yesterday brought the information that B. Starlochi (Sterlocchi) died in St Paul Sunday morning, Aug. 5, 1900 at 10 o'clock. The message came as a shock to his family and friends, as it was supposed that he was getting along well. A week before he had gone to St Paul, accompanied by his son-in-law John Briedenbach, and Father O'Hare to have a surgical operation performed for the relief of a malady for which he had suffered intensely for about five years. The surgeons performed the operation on Wednesday morning and the results appeared to be most satisfactory for a couple of days, since which, until the announcement of his death, no information had been received.

B. Starlochi was born in Como, Italy in 1825, and he came to this country about 45 years ago, his wife following a year or two later. He located at Galena, Ill. and after a year removed to Genoa, Wisconsin, where he conducted a mercantile business and managed farms until he came to Spink County SD about 16 years ago. He devoted his time here to the supervision of farming interests he acquired. He possessed fine business ability and was very successful, being worth a large amount of money at the time of his death.

His aged wife survives him and five out of the ten children born to them are living, all being daughters. Three of these ladies live in Aberdeen, namely, Mrs. John Briedenbach, Mrs. George Lupi, and Mrs. Tillie Shook, the others being Mrs. Rosa Zabolio, of Genoa, Wisconsin., and Mrs. A. Ott of Edgeley, ND.

The remains will be brought to Aberdeen this evening or tomorrow morning and the funeral will take place from Sacred Heart of Jesus Church on Tuesday forenoon at 10 o'clock.

In a history book of Aberdeen's Sacred Heart Parish published some years ago it states about B. Starlochi as follows; "An Italian gentlemen, Mr. Starlochi is given credit for supervising a fund drive to purchase a bell for the new

Sacred Heart Church. This bell was placed in the first churches frame structure. It was later moved to the new brick church, still later to the present church. It is possibly the only item from the original church that is still in use today".

Starlochi Gravestone
Aberdeen's Sacred Heart Parish Cemetery

Notes for Mary Ann "Marianna" ZABOLIO

Obit

Mrs. Mary Starlochi Expires

Passes away this Morning after a Long Illness of Pneumonia

Mrs. Mary Ann Starlochi (Marianna Zaboglio) passed away this morning at 6:30 o'clock at the residence of her daughter, Mrs. Adolph Ott, after suffering from a long attack of pneumonia. She was one of the oldest residents of the city, being at the time of her death over 81 years of age.

The funeral will be held tomorrow afternoon at the Church of the Sacred Heart at 2:30 O'clock and will be conducted by Rev. Father Dermody, pastor of the church.

The deceased was born in Northern Italy December 17, 1823. She married Bartholomew Starlochi while they lived in Italy, in 1847. They settled at Galena, Ill. where they resided for about a year and a half. They then removed to Genoa, Wisconsin where they stayed until 1884, when they removed to the extreme southern part of Brown County. About ten years ago they removed to this city. Her husband died about four years ago.

To Mr. and Mrs. Starlochi ten children were born, six daughters and four sons. All of the sons died before reaching maturity, and one daughter Mrs. John Venner, died some time ago at Genoa, Wisconsin leaving a family of seven children. The names of the children who survive their mother are Mrs. John Briedenbach of this city, Mrs. George Lupi of Minneapolis, Mrs. Albert Zabolio of Genoa,

Wisconsin, and Mrs. Adolph Ott and Mrs. Edward Shook, both of this city.

Mrs. Starlochi was a woman of much property and was well known by her many acts of charity among the needy of the city. She delighted in using her means to relieve suffering, and she won a host of friends among those to whom she administered. She was one of the foremost in the support of the Sacred Heart Church, of which she had been a member ever since she removed to Aberdeen. Everyone who knew her was drawn to her by her generous and sympathetic qualities. She will be greatly missed by the community in which she lived. She will be buried tomorrow afternoon in the Catholic Cemetery.

The following was published in the **Aberdeen Daily News** on Feb. 8, 1905 with some modifications.

The funeral of Mrs. Mary Starlochi was held yesterday afternoon at the Church of the Sacred Heart, the Rev. Father Dermody, pastor of the church officiating. The funeral was largely attended by the many friends and relatives of the deceased, all of her five living daughters being present. They are Mrs. John Briedenbach, Mrs. Adolph Ott, and Mrs. Edward Shook of this city, Mrs. George Lupi of Minneapolis and Mrs. Albert Zabolio of Genoa, Wisconsin The interment was in the Catholic Cemetery.

Birth/Death: Dates from Aberdeen Daily News obituary write up of Feb.6, 1905.

Dates for Mary Ann's Birth and death also from Ott's family Bible and birth date from scroll of the Sterlocchi family received by Rosemarie Marchetti Smith in 1997.

28. Michael[5] NICHELATTI, born in Austria; died in Austria. He married in Austria 29. (---) ANTONETTE, (Maria Antonia Chiogna) born in Austria.

Notes for Michael NICHELATTI
Name from death certificates of son John Nichelatti. Certificate filed
Vernon County register 416a.

Notes for (---) ANTONETTE (Maria Antonia **Chiogna).**
Name from son John's birth certificate. Certificate filed Vernon County
Register number 416A.

30. John[5] GABRIEL, born in Italy. He married 31. Ursula FANETTI, (Orsola Fruet) died in Italy.

Notes for John GABRIEL
Name from Margaret Gabriel Nichelatti death certificate Vernon County
Wisconsin. Register 3.

Notes for Ursula FANETTI (Orsola Fruet)

From an e-mail from Linda Flotto dated 30 Nov 2003 she has the name of Ursula as Fleek. This from notes written by her grandmother.

Generation 6

32. Michael[6] KRAUSE, born in Germany. He married unknown. (Luise Dietert)

33. Agostino Giuseppe[6] STERLOCCHI, born 18 Jul 1779 in Campodolcino, Sondrio, Italy; died 6 Sep 1850 in Italy, son of 37. Bartolomeo STERLOCCHI and 38. Domenica GHELFI. He married on 29 Jun 1812 in Italy 34. Maddalena GIANOLI, born 7 Oct 1781 in Italy; died 16 Aug 1846 in Italy.

Notes for Agostino Giuseppe STERLOCCHI
Data from e-mail prepared in Campodolcino by Augusto Sterlocchi dated July 11, 1999.

Notes for Maddalena GIANOLI
Data from e-mail prepared in Campodolcino by Augusto Sterlocchi Dated July 11, 1999

35. Francesco Giuseppe[6] ZABOGLIO, born 25 May 1801 in Sondrio, Italy; died 27 Feb 1836 in Italy, son of 39. Agostino ZABOGLIO and 40. Lucrezia GODOLA. He married on 27 Feb 1821 36. Maria Teresa Domenica Petronilla BUZZETTI, born 20 May 1797 in Vho, Sondrio,

Italy; died 10 Sep 1862 in Genoa, Vernon, Wisconsin; buried in Genoa, Vernon, Wisconsin, daughter of 41. Giovanni Battista BUZZETTI IV and 42. Marianna CERLETTI.

Notes for Francesco Giuseppe ZABOGLIO

Birth date and date of marriage from scroll of the Sterlocchi Family received by Rosemarie Marchetti Smith in 1997.

Francesco Zaboglio was the son of Agostino Zaboglio. Agostino was active in Campodolcino, Sondrio, Italy. We have found records dating the Zaboglio families activities in the area back to 1684 in the Campodolcino area. As the name was Americanized the "g" was eliminated to spell their name as Zabolio.

Like many of our ancestors Francesco Zaboglio came from Northern Italy. His homeland was in the picturesque and mountainous Alpine Region of Northern Italy. Francesco operated a stagecoach that delivered mail from Genoa, Italy through the Alps to Geneva, Switzerland. He was killed, in 1836, by an avalanche, when his youngest son John B Zabolio was 3 months old. He left a widow with five surviving children, all who were to later come to America and all settled in Genoa for at least a generation before leaving for other areas in the US. They formed and lived with the pioneers of the settlement.

Italian surnames may have been derived from geographical areas, animal names, occupations, nicknames, kinship names, or a variety of other things. Of the Genoa names Starleggia and Corti are communities near Campodolcino, Venerdi is the Italian word for Friday. Maybe someone can tell me if the name Vener has as its root been derived from Venerdi. [See Appendix D]

Notes for Maria Teresa[6] Domenica Petronilla Buzzetti

Dates of death from Mary Ann's grave marker in St Charles Cemetery, Genoa, Wisconsin. Birth date from scroll of the Sterlocchi Family received by Rosemarie Marchetti Smith in 1997.

Mary Anne's grave marker in St Charles Cemetery is marked with the name of Mary A Zabolio. But the name given to her at hcr at Baptism in Italy was Maria Teresa Domencia Petronilla Buzzetti. She came to the US, as a widow, prior to 1860 with her youngest son, John. Maria on 1 June 1860 was issued title through the Homestead Act of 40 acres of land of the North East Quarter of the South West Quarter of Section 28 in what is now Genoa Township. This quarter section contains the St Charles Cemetery where Maria lies today. She in fact has the dubious honor of having the oldest grave in the St Charles Cemetery. As the first recorded Mass in Genoa was said just two days after her death, in all probability it was her Funeral Mass. This Mass was said at the home of her daughter Mary Ann Starlochi by the Rev. Lucien Galtier from Prairie du Chien. The Starlochis owned a stone home south of where the Bank in Genoa is today.

Generation 7

37. Bartolomeo[7] STERLOCCHI, born 1741 in Italy; died 11 Nov 1813 in Italy, son of 43. Guglielmo STERLOCCHI and 44. Maria Caterina BUZZETTI. He married (1) on 25 Feb 1767 in Italy 38. Domenica GHELFI, born in Italy; died in Italy; (2) Anna Maria GHELFI; (3) on 13 Apr 1790 Maria GIANERA.

Notes for Bartolomeo STERLOCCHI
Data from e-mail prepared in Campodolcino by Augusto Sterlocchi Dated July 11, 1999

Notes for Domenica GHELFI
Data from e-mail prepared in Campodolcino by Augusto Sterlocchi Dated July 11, 1999

39. Agostino[7] ZABOGLIO, born 9 Sep 1776 in Italy; died 30 Mar 1803 in Italy, son of 45. Antonio F Zaboglio and 46. Annamaria P GUANELLA. He married (1) on 19 Feb 1800 in Italy 40. Lucrezia GODOLA, born 9 Apr 1778 in Italy; died 15 Jun 1803 in Italy; (2) on 20 Jul 1807 in Italy Agosti MARTA.

41. Giovanni Battista[7] BUZZETTI IV, born 2 Feb 1763 in Vho, Sondria, Italy; died 6 Jun 1820 in Mese, Sondrio, Italy, son of 47. Giovanni Battista BUZZETTI III and 48. Domenica ADAMOSSI. He married 42. Marianna CERLETTI, born 13 Mar 1767 in San Bernardo, Sondrio,

Italy; died 5 Nov 1833 in Vho, Sondria, Italy, daughter of 49. Teresa FALCINELLA.

Notes for Giovanni Battista BUZZETTI IV
Data from scroll prepared in Campodolcino but not able to verify from the US.

Notes for Marianna CERLETTI
Data from scroll prepared in Campodolcino but not able to verify from the US.

Generation 8

43. Guglielmo[8] STERLOCCHI, born before 1707 in Italy; died before 1784 in Italy, son of 50. Antonio STERLOCCHI. He married on 4 Oct 1727 in Campodolcino, Sondrio, Italy 44. Maria Caterina BUZZETTI.

Notes for Guglielmo STERLOCCHI
Data from e-mail prepared in Campodolcino by Augusto Sterlocchi Dated July 11, 1999

Notes for Maria Caterina BUZZETTI
Data from scroll prepared in Campodolcino but not able to verify from the US.

45. Antonio[8] F Zaboglio, born 2 Mar 1754 in Italy; died 24 Aug 1830 in Italy, son of 51. Agostino ZABOGLIO and 52. Caterina GHELFI. He married (1) 46. Annamaria P GUANELLA, born 1744 in Italy; died 5 Aug 1793 in Italy; (2) on 20 Jul 1807 Agosti MARTA.

47. Giovanni Battista[8] BUZZETTI III, born 27 May 1730 in Vho, Sondria, Italy, son of 53. Giovanni Battista BUZZETTI II and 54. Maria GIANOTTI. He married on 20 Aug 1758 48. Domenica ADAMOSSI, born in Lirone, Sondrio, Italy.

Notes for Giovanni Battista BUZZETTI III
Data from scroll prepared in Campodolcino but not able to verify from the US.

Notes for Domenica ADAMOSSI
Data from scroll prepared in Campodolcino but not able to verify from the US.

49. Teresa[8] FALCINELLA, born in Italy. She married unknown.

Generation 9

50. Antonio[9] STERLOCCHI, died about 1745, son of 55. Guglielmo STERLOCCHI and 56. Maria Caterina POLETTA. He married unknown.

Notes for Antonio STERLOCCHI

Data from e-mail prepared in Campodolcino by Augusto Sterlocchi Dated July 11, 1999

51. Agostino[9] ZABOGLIO, died 1791 in Italy. He married on 17 Aug 1741 in Italy 52. Caterina GHELFI, born in Italy; died 25 Oct 1776 in Italy.

53. Giovanni Battista[9] BUZZETTI II, born 12 Aug 1706 in Vho, Sondria, Italy, son of 57. Giovanni Battista BUZZETTI I and 58. Lucrezia GIAMBELLI. He married on 18 Nov 1728 54. Maria GIANOTTI.

Notes for Giovanni Battista BUZZETTI II
Data from scroll prepared in Campodolcino but not able to verify from the US.

Generation 10

55. Guglielmo[10] STERLOCCHI, son of 59. Antonio STERLOCCHI. He married on 23 Jul 1669 56. Maria Caterina POLETTA.

Notes for Guglielmo STERLOCCHI
Data from e-mail prepared in Campodolcino by Augusto Sterlocchi Dated July 11, 1999

Notes for Maria Caterina POLETTA
Data from e-mail prepared in Campodolcino by Augusto Sterlocchi Dated July 11, 1999

57. Giovanni Battista[10] BUZZETTI I, born 1 Jul 1677 in Cimaganda, Sondrio, Italy, son of 60. Giovanni BUZZETTI. He married 58. Lucrezia GIAMBELLI.

Notes for Giovanni Battista BUZZETTI I
Data from scroll prepared in Campodolcino but not able to verify from the US.

Notes for Lucrezia GIAMBELLI
Data from scroll prepared in Campodolcino but not able to verify from the US.

Generation 11

59. Antonio[11] STERLOCCHI, born before 1600, son of 61. Giovanni BATTISTA Sterlocchi. He married unknown.

Notes for Antonio STERLOCCHI
Data from e-mail prepared in Campodolcino by Augusto Sterlocchi Dated July 11, 1999

60. Giovanni[11] BUZZETTI, son of 62. Giacoma BUZZETTI. He married unknown.

Generation 12

61. Giovanni[12] BATTISTA Sterlocchi, died before 1641, son of 63. Donato Battista STERLOCCHI. He married unknown.

Notes for Giovanni Battista STERLOCCHI
Data from e-mail prepared in Campodolcino by Augusto Sterlocchi Dated July 11, 1999

62. Giacoma[12] BUZZETTI, son of 64. Antonio BUZZETTI. He married unknown.

Generation 13

63. Donato[13] Battista STERLOCCHI. He married unknown.

Notes for Donato Battista STERLOCCHI
Data from e-mail prepared in Campodolcino by Augusto Sterlocchi Dated July 11, 1999

64. Antonio[13] BUZZETTI, born 1569. He married unknown.

APPENDIX B

The Chroniclers

Many people spent time and personal resources to research the history of the family of our epic. There were (and are) no generals, dukes, or princes—no industrial magnates, political leaders, reputed authors, or inventors. Yet the diligent work of the chroniclers whose stories you are about to read have uncovered thousands of living relatives as well as more than 480 ancestors of the writer. All were inconspicuous, ordinary, and remarkably unremarkable. Ines Curti (aka Sister de Sales, FSPA), daughter of Elizabeth Malin-Curti, began it all by researching the history of her mother's family and privately publishing her research in 1976. She traced the family back from Sharpsburg, Pennsylvania, to Gofis, Austria. Her initial successes encouraged Jean Pedretti Flottmeyer (daughter of Albert Pedretti, son of Maggie Malin), who focused on compiling lists of the descendants of Josef Anton Malin and his wife, Margaret Guentner. As her interest spread, she discovered records in America leading to identifying the family's oldest immigrant, Maria Teresa Dominica Zaboglio (nee Buzzetti). James Venner opened the door wide when he connected the dots of Buzzetti, Zaboglio, Venner, and Starlochi back to Campodolcino and began correspondence with Augusto Sterlocchi in Campodolcino, who provided valuable confirmation of preliminary research and contacts with others in the area. Soon Campodolcino natives Luigi Fanetti, Felice Ghelfi, Dino Buzzetti, and Paulo Via were engaged in the search to link the families of Genoa, Wisconsin, to their historical background in Val San Giacomo.

Independent of their work, Suzanne Pedretti (daughter of Joseph Pedretti, son of Stephen Pedretti, son of Stefano Pedretti), who had relocated to Cincinnati, Ohio, engaged in the search when she was approached by Dottie Walters, an art historian who was writing a book about the Pedretti fresco artists who lived in and worked out of Cincinnati. Following a variety of leads, she headed toward a place called San Bernardo in Sondrio, Lombardy. Luck led her to run into Alberto Cerletti, who was visiting San Bernardo the day she arrived and is a serious amateur genealogist. He was able to show Suzanne the records maintained by the local church documenting the births of her great-grandfather Stefano Pedretti and his two brothers who immigrated to Genoa with him in 1854.

In 2009 I traveled to Campodolcino, and in preparation for my visit, Luigi Fanetti and Alberto Cerletti engaged the help of Felice Gelfi and Dino Buzzetti to surprise me with more than double the number of known ancestors. Since then, with their help and the use of ever-growing documentation available at a variety of websites, we now have identified 488 ancestors of the forty double cousins who can claim both Peter Pedretti and Tom Venner as their grandfathers.

Unless noted otherwise, the stories of these historians are told in their own words. I asked each person to tell why they found genealogy so interesting and what they had learned through their research. When I was unable to obtain their autobiographical sketches, I wrote as accurately about their contributions as I could. The chroniclers are listed in alphabetical order.

Buzzetti, Dino

(Written in 2010)

My interest in this research was mainly passed on to me by my father, who used to tell me episodes that happened to family members—to my father's father and to his mother, Gianera, and even to his grandmother Silvani.

These episodes related to:

Father's great-uncle Buzzetti, who was an Austrian gendarme (at the time the Austrians were our conquerors) who was executed by the Austrians in 1848 for reasons that I wanted to understand.

Father's uncle, Buzzetti Gioacchino, who immigrated to America in 1888 but of whom there has been no more news since 1936.

A relative of Father's grandmother (Silvani John), who immigrated to London and made a noteworthy fortune. He was a great benefactor and upon his death left all his relatives so much money that father's grandmother was able to build a three-story house with electricity in 1864—one of the first with this innovation.

The incredible story about a family head called Torricelli, who married in Gallivaggio in 1816. His offspring were to become my mother's family, but no one had ever heard of him before.

I began to collect information more to assuage my ꭐriosity, accessing the archives of churches and municipalities. It was necessary to gain more information about the factors that influenced the tribulations of families over the centuries, like political events, dominions, the border lines, migrations, and so on. One such factor was sustenance, which was mainly from agriculture, especially sheep farming; another was the dependence on transport as a source of revenue in Val San Giacomo from South of the Alps to the North (central Europe), which disappeared from 1885 onwards. Others included industrialization, historical events, wars, natural events like floods and landslides (the Buzzettis lost everything they had in Vhò and scattered all over the Valley to start off again from scratch in 1834), and complicated events involving the families themselves.

All these interesting factors motivated my research in genealogy. I slowly resolved all the above-mentioned "curiosities". Nevertheless, my interest continues to increase and to spread to more families and to a vaster territory.

I have met other people with the same interests (Luigi Fanetti, Felice Ghelfi, Alberto Cerletti, and others), creating a bond of collaboration: each for his own territory, his own ability and knowledge, scientific or personal. Luigi, in particular, with his knowledge of computer programs and use of the Internet, has let me to meet descendants of Italian families living abroad.

An example is Anthony Buzzetti, who has been in contact with me since 1998 and has permitted me to meet members of his family who have even come to Italy. I have met descendants of Italian families who live in Genoa, Wisconsin: Jim Venner, Anthony Buzzetti, and their numerous relatives (I won't list them all so as not to forg any). Through Anthony I learnt much about my relative Buzzetti Gioacchino, who immigrated to Nevada. It is all because of this that I dedicate so much time and attention to genealogy.

Many of those from new Genoa originally came from Val San Giacomo, and, as you well know, each comes from a different village but their destinies are intertwined. Information must be gathered from the archives of local churches (handwritten and in a single, jealously guarded copy). Collaboration is necessary.

As far as the Pedretti family is concerned, originally from San Bernardo, there no longer seems to be any trace of them there. There is, though, a significant presence in Chiavenna, Gordona, and Sondrio—so much so that I did not believe they had origins in San Bernardo. Luigi deserves to take the credit for the research done on the Pedretti family; my help was marginal. It was, though, an important opportunity for me to learn many things, to meet you, and to inspire important, positive developments.

Best wishes and . . . arrivederci!

Dino

Buzzetti, Anthony

(Written by author)

Tony Buzzetti lives in Columbia, South Carolina, and has from time to time supplied Jim Venner with vital information and contacts related to the origins of the Buzzetti family. Tony's great-great-grandfather Pietro Antonio Silvestro Buzzetti born on December 21, 1809, was the sister of our great-great-great-grandmother, Maria Teresa Dominica Petronilla Buzzetti, the oldest known cestor in our story who came to America. It was through work of Tony and his distant relative, Dino Buzzetti that ▪arned about the ancestors of Maria Teresa

▪rletti, Alberto
(written in May 2010)

The study of history by reading historical books relating to all villages of Valchiavenna, I started almost forty years ago. I've always been attracted by local history: the most ancient documents, preserved in historical archives dating back almost a thousand years ago.

I am a member of an association that studies history, the Centre for Historical Studies of Valchiavenna. This association annually sends a newsletter to all members that consists of an average of three hundred pages and ten chapters, each chapter written by an author who has made an historical research archive that might relate to many different events: the story of a village, the passage of armies in our valley, disputes with the bishops of Como for the payment of fees, conflicts over the borders of Valchiavenna and the surrounding areas, and other interesting stories. This association also publishes books relating to important historical research.

I started doing research about fifteen years ago when I retired and therefore had more time; I was able to "vent" my passion. The first search I did was about the origins of the Cerletti family, from documents available at the historical state archive of Sondrio; I found the first traces of the Cerletti in the second half of fifteenth century. Documents I consulted included ancient books (registers) that collected deeds relating to transfers of ownership. ▪

these acts are mentioned the names of buyers and sellers. Reading these deeds carefully, you can create a genealogic tree.

To get to this first result, I spent whole days at the State Archives of Sondrio to consult records, and sometimes I would stay till the evening and not have found anything that interested me. But my passion for research about my ancestors always encouraged me to continue. Often I had to ask the help of experts to interpret correctly what was written, as the writings of those times were not easy to read.

Then I moved to the historical archive of the Church of S. Bernardo, where the records begin in the second half of seventeenth century—records of baptisms, marriages, and deaths. The first thing I did, in agreement with the administrators of the church, was an inventory of all documents, records, etc., and a proper reordering of the whole archive. Then I consulted the records for baptisms, marriages, and deaths, where are cited the names of parents, so I was able to draw a family tree. The first family tree that I did was that of my family.

The administrators of the church knew my passion for historical and genealogical research, so when descendants came to S. Bernardo asking for news of their ancestors, they referred them to me. Over the years I have done research about Cerletti family members living in Milan, Switzerland, and the United States (California and Wisconsin); the Gadolas in Uruguay; the Barinis and the Paiarolas in Switzerland; the Pedrettis in Germany; and the Pedretti-Cerletti families for our friend Mike, in collaboration with our friends Felice and Dino.

While consulting records I have discovered important things, but I was particularly impressed that by the second half of the seventeenth century, men emigrating from S. Bernardo seasonally to Italian cities in neighboring Switzerland, then Germany and France, traveled hundreds of miles on foot. These people were paid with coins that were used in those places, so the accounting records of the church have records of a dozen different currencies. I wonder how they computed evaluations of values between one currency and another for the exchange, because the level of education was low if not nonexistent. But surely there was a way to change money.

Another bit of information that struck me is about the history of the statue of Our Lady that is located right above the altar as you enter the church. In the second half of the eighteenth century, people of Saint Bernard had commissioned the statue from neighboring Switzerland, to be crafted by artisans skilled in the construction of statues especially for churches. When the statue was finished, people had to carry the statue to S. Bernardo; the path from the location where it was built (Disentis, Grisons) was quite long, at least three days on foot, with the statue carried the whole way on the shoulders of four people.

The young people of Saint Bernard—our ancestors— chose the more difficult and arduous path through the mountains. Why? To avoid paying taxes!! When the young people, about fifteen of them, descended from the mountain, all the people at the center of the village welcomed them, and there was a big party.

The attachment I have for my homeland is strong, and as time passes, the more I try to know the past: I search particularly on older homes or stables, for engravings of ancient dates on the roof beams or on wooden or stone arches above the entrance doors.

Dear friends and kin from America, this is my story about the passion to know the origins of the village, the origins of people who have settled, how they lived, and all the events that have occurred.

Curti, Ines (Sister De Sales)

(Written by James Venner)

Ines Elisabeth Curti, a Franciscan Sister of Perpetual Adoration, knew members of the Malin family who still lived in Pennsylvania and used their help to find the marriage certificate of her grandfather F. Josef Malin and Margaret Marie Guentner and the birth certificates of their two oldest children, Margaret Marie and Paul, in the church records at St. Mary, Sharpsburg, Pennsylvania. There she found that her grandfather was baptized in a church in Gofis, Austria. Using her religious connections, she was able to verify his birth records. In 1976 she distributed a document presenting her research.

Ines's experience would be repeated for other branches of the family. By 1970, little to nothing was known about the histories of people who settled in Genoa, Wisconsin. Memories were terribly short, and it has only been through the diligent pursuit of this family's past by Ines and later members of the next generation that any records have been recovered. This amnesia about the past seems to have been endemic in the first half of the twentieth century. Was it that descendants of Axis countries in particular did not want their neighbors to know of their ethnic heritage, or was it the inevitable loss of interest in peoples who immigrate and fight hard to establish a foothold in the new land? We know the gentry maintained their wealth of knowledge about their ancestors, but the time or interest did not and maybe could not exist in the class of people we celebrate in this work. Ines, with the leisure afforded a nun, could pursue our story in a way most of her generation who were still struggling to eke a living out of the land could have if they had the interest. In a country and a time when each individual, unless born into wealth, had to work from dawn to dusk, there was little time, need, or inclination to maintain ties with a past that was in a faraway land. Ines ignited an interest in her family, and that interest has continued to grow to this very day as the world gets smaller, data is easier to access, and more members of this family find a few hours of leisure available.

Fanetti, Luigi
(Written in 2010)

My name is Gregorio Luigi Fanetti. I'm sixty-one, and I have always lived in Campodolcino, in the province of Sondrio, Lombardy, Italy. I have developed an interest in genealogy over the past thirty years. Why did I begin? Probably because I had only ever known one grandmother. Caterina Guanella was a splendid person, and the fond memory of her made me want to find out more about my ancestors, the most significant moments of their lives, and the people and places they associated with. Since 1550 all my children's ancestors (over 750 of them) were born in Valchiavenna except for one, who came from Saxony (Germany).

In Italy, genealogical research was traditionally carried out only by historians and by nobility looking for illustrious relatives. In the 1980s I bought a series of books dealing with genealogical research, but all of them dealt at length on noble titles and the differences between heraldic coats of arms or escutcheons. I was, and still am, quite content to find out about more modest relatives, who are just as important to my family even if they are not as illustrious.

At the beginning I collected documents, photographs, and letters and made a brief description of each one. With the advent of the first computers (mine was a Spectrum Sinclair), I began to insert the data I had in chronological order. I was not yet able to process images, though. With newer computers and software, using Excel I slowly built up a family tree going back five generations. The Internet gave me the possibility of making contact with people who had emigrated from Campodolcino and were trying to trace their origins. So I widened my research to include more and more families.

Through the Internet I learnt about specific programs like Gedcom, which gave my research a boost and enabled me to process the data I downloaded. What in the past were mere handwritten notes or files containing details regarding one single person now became links between parents, brothers, spouses, and offspring.

Acquiring the ability to scan old photographs gave me the possibility of not only working on documents but linking them to images, people, and dates. The endless hours I spent at the computer doing all this wouldn't have been possible without the understanding and help of my wife, Giuseppina Levi (who has always wanted to know why

ıer typically Jewish surname has been present in our valley
ɔr over four centuries) and friends like Dino Buzzetti,
ɛlice Ghelfi, and Walter Trussoni.

With Dino and Felice's help, I read and transcribed
many registers, which were then copied as data on the
computer. I don't know how many times we clashed with
my wife who insisted in adding the names of the many
babies who died soon after birth, to honor their mothers
who suffered giving birth to them. This information,
though, is not determining as far as genealogy is concerned.

We consulted municipal registers, which have only
been obligatory since 1861, that keep a record of births,
weddings, deaths, and family status. For periods before that
date we researched parishes. Since the Council of Trento in
the mid-1500s, parishes have had to keep registers: one was
called the *Register of the Souls*, which had to record the
names of the baptized, the confirmed, the married, and the
dead, as well as a periodic *State of the Souls* (similar to the
current certificate giving details of a household) recording
which sacrament had been given to each family member.
The first registers found in our parishes, though, only date
back to the early 1600s.

Reading municipal registers printed in Italian is
completely different from reading the parish ones entirely
handwritten and in Latin. Every priest has his own way of
keeping records: some wrote lengthy preliminary remarks
then forgot essential information. You can find peculiarities
in baptismal registers: after the classical formula "natum est
ex." some had the names of the father and the mother,
others preferred the name of the mother, married to . . .

Nowadays, on a birth certificate, you can find recorded all details pertaining to that person (matrimony, divorce, death, etc.), but that did not occur in church registers, so it was difficult to find other information for that person (like their wedding date, to whom, date of death, and so on). Brides were identified by their fathers' names, and age was given as the number of years "ciciter annorum."

The relatively few surnames and names have caused a lot of wasted time and sometimes make it impossible to continue the research of a family tree. We've often been unable to associate families because we've found parents and children with the same names. Once it was normal to give a firstborn son the name of his paternal grandfather, and the other sons would be given the names of the other grandfathers. Children were often named for the patron saint of the parish. All this has caused many cases of homonyms.

Reading handwritten registers, often written in barely legible handwriting, was often made even more indecipherable thanks to the abbreviations used. Dino and Felice are much more expert in this than I am.

Unfortunately, not all parish registers in the Valley have been well kept, and some have disappeared, even recently. I personally retrieved twenty or so registers (paying for them) from the parishes of Olmo and San Bernardo that a private collector had. Other books have pages missing, probably torn out by people who wanted to eliminate traces of an ancestor. Obviously, when pages or entire periods are missing from a register, the continuity of the research is interrupted. This is when you curse those who haven't kept the records well and especially the thieves.

Something that really needs to be done in all archives is to store all documents in computers to guarantee the preservation of the information they contain without having to hand over originals.

Here is a curious thing I have learned. Many people study their family name with reference only to the paternal surname; I have instead considered all branches, thus finding out that if my children consider, for example, both parents, they are 50 percent Fanetti and 50 percent Levi; their grandparents, they are 25 percent Fanetti and 75 percent Levi; four great-grandparents, they are 7.1 percent Fanetti, 14.3 percent Levi, 28.6 percent Trussoni, 10.7 percent Guanella + others; five great-grandparents, they are 2.2 percent Fanetti, 8.7 percent Levi, 8.7 percent Guanella, 8.7 percent Ghelfi, 8.7 percent Curti, and 23.9 percent Trussoni.

It's evident that searching only the paternal side is limiting.

The town I live in has about one thousand inhabitants, but in my computer network I have gathered and connected twenty thousand people belonging to families who have lived or emigrated from Campodolcino.

In Italy and in Europe, there is a law that protects all personal data and that forbids the publication of personal information for all living people or those deceased less than 70 years ago. This law does not permit me to publish my work or the results of my research. Even if I have posted various family trees to North and South America and to Australia, I cannot do so in Europe.

Ghelfi, Felice

My name is Felice Ghelfi. I was born in Prestone, a subdivision of Campodolcino, on May 2, 1936, to Francesco Mario Ghelfi and Lidia Prima Fanetti. I've always been interested in local history. At age fifteen I read *The Countryside of Chiavenna* by G. B. Crollalanza, which I found interesting. At first I thought that the facts relating to the early Roman era until the year 1200 were pretty romanticized, but then I found them credible and interesting, partly because it is still possible to trace the names of various places mentioned by the author, confirmed by the stories passed down to me by our ancestors.

As for genealogy, I became interested in it after rummaging in a large trunk in my grandparents' house in Preston, where I found a request from the faiths of the birth of my ancestor James Gadola (12/01/1806–08/04/1878) addressed to the Provost of S. Don Giovanni Battista Campodolcino Jeremiah Piccinelli in 1866, which I attach to the end of this letter. (Will genealogy be a family vice?)

Once I was on business for several years (about 35) away from Campodolcino. When I returned to my native country, and thanks to Louis and Walter who directed the use of the computer, I started my research. I had the opportunity to access the parish and municipal archives Campodolcino. I am committed to reading the often-difficult records of baptism, marriages, and deaths, and now I find myself with data from over 20,000 Campodolcinesi recorded in various archives and listed on my computer. Now with the help of photographic technology and the precious common interest of Luigi and Dino and the great friendship between us, I hope to continue this research, which gives me great satisfaction even if I start worrying that my sight is becoming more scarce.

For those who can read Italian:

Mi chiamo Ghelfi Felice, sono nato, a Prestone frazione di Campodolcino il 02/ 05/ 1936 da Ghelfi Francesco Mario e Fanetti Lidia Prima

Per la verità sono sempre stato interessato alla storia locale, a 15 anni ho avuto modo di leggere "Il Contado di Chiavenna" di G.B. Crollalanza che ho trovato interessantissimo. Pensavo che i fatti relativi ai primi anni dell'epoca Romana sino agli anni 1200 fossero piuttosto romanzati, poi li ho trovati credibili e molto interessanti, anche perché è ancora oggi possibile rintracciare i nomi delle diverse località citate dall'Autore, confermate dalle storie raccontatemi dai nostri vecchi.

Per quanto riguarda la genealogia ho cominciato ad interessarmi dopo che rovistando in una grande cassapanca nella casa dei miei nonni a Prestone ho trovato una richiesta delle fedi di nascita di un mio antenato Gadola Giacomo 12/ 01/ 1806 / 08/ 04/ 1878 rivolta al Prevosto di S. Giovanni Battista di Campodolcino Don Geremia Piccinelli nel 1866 che allego alla fine (La genealogia sarà un vizio di famiglia?)

Dopo che per motivi di lavoro sono stato per parecchi anni (circa 35) lontano da Campodolcino sono ritornato al paese natio e grazie a Luigi e Walter che mi hanno indirizzato nell'uso del computer, ho iniziato le mie ricerche. Ho avuto la possibilità di accedere agli archivi parrocchiali e comunali di Campodolcino, mi sono impegnato alla lettura per la verità molte volte difficoltosa dei registri di battesimo, matrimoni e morti,e ora mi ritrovo con i dati di oltre 20.000 Campodolcinesi registrati nei vari archivi e riportati sul mio computer

Adesso anche con l'aiuto della tecnologia della fotografia e del prezioso comune interesse di Luigi e Dino nonché del grande rapporto di amicizia che intercorre tra di noi spero di continuare queste ricerche, che mi danno una grande soddisfazione anche se comincio a preoccuparmi per la mia vista che si fa sempre più scarsa.

Pedretti-Flottmeyer, Jean

I was always interested in genealogy, but it was not until my children were in school that I got serious about it. I started by checking out courthouse records. One thing led to another. I found Stefano and Adelaide's wedding certificate, among other things. The more I found, the more obsessed I became.

I found stuff about Starlochi-Zabolio members, but I had a hard time accepting Zabolios as part of the family. Why wouldn't someone know if Zabolios were part of our background? Besides, Mom's aunt Rosa married a Zabolio. Finally I worked up enough courage to call and meet with Annabel Zabolio. Before that I didn't know Annabel or how I'd be received. Annabel was delightful, and it turned out to be a smart move.

Annabel told me she had an old family album but claimed she didn't know several people in it. As I paged through the album, Annabel talked about what she knew and believed about the family. Much of it sounded familiar.

The pieces fit remarkably well. I left telling Annabel I needed to run some of this before Mom and see what she thought.

A short time later, Annabel called and insisted I come to her place and explain what we had discovered to someone coming from California. It turned out to be Rosemarie Smith, the granddaughter of Josie Starlochi Ott and a niece of my great-grandmother Mary Madeline Venner. It was a fun day. Annabel and Rosemarie were discussing making risot as I left for La Crosse.

We weren't done yet. I came in contact with Jim Venner and a few others. The end result was *From Campodolcino to Genoa.*

Finding that Maria Teresa Zaboglio was my four-times grandmother was probably my biggest discovery.

Pedretti, Suzanne
(Written by author)

Suzanne was the first person from Genoa, Wisconsin to rediscover the birthplace of Stefano Maria Pedretti, who is the progenitor of all Genoa Pedrettis. Stephen's tombstone in Saint Charles Cemetery in Genoa, Wisconsin clearly stated his birthplace as Saint Barnard, Italy; however, none of his descendants had been able to locate Saint Barnard or Saint Bernard on a map of Italy. Some family members speculated that Stephen's birthplace had been in the Great Saint Bernard Pass area, but maps showed no town there or anywhere else in Italy which translated into English as Saint Barnard or Saint Bernard.

Susanne was living in Cincinnati, the home of the famous nineteenth-century Pedretti fresco artists. Dottie

Walters, an art historian writing a book on the Pedretti artists who lived in Cincinnati in the 1800s, contacted Susanne and then put her in touch with Ladina (Pedretti) Jaecklin, living in Ennetbaden, Switzerland. Ladina, a relative of the Pedretti artists, has a strong interest in Pedretti family history. She had traced her own Pedretti history back to 1531 to the Mountain of San Bernardo, which lies above Chiavenna, Italy. However, she had not traveled to the mountain. In August of 1996, Suzanne and Lavina traveled together to San Bernardo and arrived a few days before the annual celebration of the most important holiday for the town, the Assumption. The holiday attracts many former residents of San Bernardo, and luckily Alberto Cerletti, the foremost San Bernardo genealogist and historian, was visiting. When Suzanne inquired about the Pedretti family, Cerletti opened the church and found the documents that recorded the birth of Stefano and his brother Sylvester. She discovered that Stefano was the second child of fifteen born to Guglielmo Pedretti (born April 17, 1804) and Maria Teresa Cerletti.

Finally, the family knew where to look, although no one traveled there for further research until I journeyed there in 2009. In anticipation of my visit, Alberto Cerletti, with help from Luigi Fanetti and Dino Buzzetti, combed through the San Bernardo historical Books of the Souls and traced our family back to Guglielmo Pedretti, the father of Giuseppe Pedretti who was born in 1654. By also tracing spouses and their ancestors, Cerletti traced our linage back to Laurenti Zerletti who was born near the end of the fourteenth century.

Sterlocchi, Augusto

Jim Venner's first human contact in Campodolcino was Augusto Sterlocchi, who had done some research on the Sterlocchi family. Even more important, he put Jim in touch with Luigi Fanetti and Paolo Via.

Venner, James Francis

I guess I always had a bit of interest in family history. When I was a high school kid shredding corn for our next-door neighbors, the Guanellas, Eugenia Gianoli Guanella (Jean) told me that she thought that the Venners and the Gianolis were related to each other somehow. It had to be a Saturday or the Thanksgiving weekend, as I was not in school. Well she was proven right, but it took years to find this out. I went to school with Frank G.'s kids, but we were not aware of any relationship. Anyway, I told Jean that the Venners that were married to the Pedrettis were related since Mary Malin was married to Tony Gianoli, but I didn't know of any other relationship. She said that someday she was going to find how the Venners and Gianoli families were related. Of course, this was my first genealogy mistake. I wish that was the only genealogy mistake I made. Other mistakes I made included thinking that Stephen P. and Adelaide were probably an arranged marriage. Another was where the Pedrettis came from. We know what the grave marker says they came from Saint Bernard. Since we could never find a village named Saint Bernard in Italy, I looked around the Saint Bernard Pass areas, greater and minor, for a settlement by that name.

I didn't do much with genealogy until the 1980s. Then personal computers had become available. I started by putting the information in for the immediate family, then working up to the uncles and aunts and grandparents and extended family members. One thing that makes it easy for me was the fact most everyone in our family is buried in the Saint Charles Cemetery in Genoa. Few others delving into family history had the preponderance of ancestors buried in but one cemetery. I thought that I would write a family history of the Venner and Pedretti families after I retired. In 1996 I started to put a family history book together. When I got into the book, I soon found that I could move back in time easily. In fact, I could get the roots of the book back into Northern Italy. That was when I expanded the title to *Campodolcino to Genoa*. It is fascinating that whole families from the Valchiavenna area, over a few years, moved in mass to Genoa.

These original immigrants were remarkable people. They were the first of what later proved to be a huge wave of Italian immigrants coming to the United States. History books say that only 10,000 Italians were living in the US in 1860. Our ancestors were among the first. It also points out that our ancestors lived in an area with very limited resources. Until around 1850 it was necessary for the men to go off to other areas of Europe to earn a living, at least in the wintertime. Around 1850 they started to come to the Americas, both north and south.

One of the discoveries I found was that L. Cerletti (1725–1759), one of our ancestors who married Teresa Falcinella, had children that are on the ancestral path of both the Pedretti family line and also of the Venner family lines. Thus when our parents Pedrettis married a Venner they were marrying fourth cousins once removed. I'm sure that they never knew it.

I have always found family members willing to assist with information. No one knew where the Sterlocchi family of our great-great-grandparents had disappeared to. Al Levi thought that they had moved to South Dakota. I wrote a note to a South Dakota genealogy group, and within a couple of weeks they sent back a copy of Bart and Mary Ann's obituary that located when they died and where they are buried. Family members and friends have always been willing to help with information. I shouldn't start listing names as I'm sure that I will overlook numerous names of people who also helped. Here in no special order are the names of people who provided data for the database.

Dr. John Vener and Tracy Vener of the Minnesota Vener family made trips to Italy and brought information back.

Of course, Paolo Via, who provided historic data and background information on our families' original homeland. Also, Dino Buzzetti provided names, data, and dates for many individuals who went back to Italy to see our ancestral homeland.

Charles Hebert, a descendant of John Battista Zabolio, also visited Italy.

Annabel Zabolio had inherited the scrapbook on the Zabolio family with pictures, funeral cards on the members, and copies of obituaries.

Rosemarie Smith visited Italy and found additional data.

Eugenia Gianoli Guanella, with Lucy Eugenia Saft Jankord and Catherine Francoli Clinton, helped with the Francoli and Gianoli families' history.

Tony Buzzetti did much work on the Zaboglio and Buzzetti families. I'm quite sure that he also visited our ancestral homeland.

Now I'm sure I missed a gross of other names who provided information.

Via, Paolo

Paolo Via has become one of the foremost experts on the history and development of Val San Giacomo. Before he retired, he was a teacher and played a role in increasing the availability of education to all citizens of the valley and in upgrading the level of education. He has studied the dialects and history of the area and is especially knowledgeable about the migration of Campodolcino families to various parts of the world, particularly about the substantial migration to Genoa, Wisconsin.

APPENDIX C

Meaning of Surnames—Pedretti and Vener

Pedretti

We know that those who carry the name Pedretti and are descendants of the San Bernardo Pedretti family received their name from Guglielmo Gadola, the son of Pietro Gadola. Guglielmo reportedly performed an act of bravery in early 1500s that earned him the honor of selecting a new surname to be used in perpetuity by his offspring. He chose to honor his father by taking on the name Son of Pietro, which in Italian is Pedretto. Early in the next century the name had evolved to Pedretti, the plural of Pedretto. Pedretti can mean many Pedrettos or the children of Pietro. I present some different theories of sources for the surname below.

Northern Italian: patronymic from a pet form of the personal name Pietro.

The surname PEDRO is of twofold origin, meaning a large stone or pedestal. It was originally rendered in the Latin form PETRO. The name was extremely popular throughout Christian Europe in the Middle Ages, as it had been bestowed by Christ as a byname on the apostle Simon bar Jonah, the brother of Andrew. The name was chosen for its symbolic significance and is a translation of the Aramaic *kefa*, meaning a rock. Saint Peter is regarded as the founding father of the Christian Church, and in Christian Germany in the fourteenth century, Petrus (Peter) was the most frequent given name. The name was also occasionally used as a topographic name for someone who lived on a patch of stony soil or by a large outcrop of rock, originally rendered in ancient documents in the Latin form PETRA. It may also be a metonymic occupational name for a quarryman or stone-carver. The name has traveled widely and taken many forms.

"The (San Bernardo) strain of Pedretti derives from Gadola. In 1559 (there is a record of) 'John and William as Pedretto dela Gadola of St. Bernard in Val San Giacomo.' The shape of the name at the end of the sixteenth century was Pedretto, always accompanied by Gadola. Only in the 17th century took the current form, as is attested in 1641 Sylvester was the son of Christopher Pedretti. At about this time some members of the Pedretti family moved from San Bernardo to Chiavenna, Samòlaco and Gordona." (The information is from the State Archives of Sondrio, Notary, volumes 1006, 1542, 1837, and 5099 as written in Valchiavenna monthly information, sport and culture Year IX – n. 10 - 10 October 1989)

Gadola

In legal documents of 1463 and 1464, it appears Giovanni dela Gadola of Scannabecco was also known as William of Filigheccio. Evidently the family that moved from Filigheccio to Scannabecco, better known today as San Rocco, took the new surname. In turn, the dela Gadola family split into several branches, including those of Pedretto and Gianera, The surname Gadola is probably matronymic origin, deriving from the personal name Agatha, as in the daughter of Agata but altered over time. Possible evolution Agatola, Gatola, Gadola.

Numerological Meaning of Pedretti

"You have a power of expression, either in speaking or writing. You are in favor for studying and research. You are clever, clear-sighted and intellectual. You don't like to let others know your true feelings. You might be atheistic or agnostic. You have an eventful, exciting life. You are versatile and have the ability to learn easily.

"You are very intuitive. You have a reservoir of inspired wisdom combined with inherited analytical ability, which could reward you through expressions of spiritual leadership, business analysis, marketing, artistic visions, and scientific research. Operating on spiritual side of your individuality can bring you to the great heights, and drop you off if you neglect your spiritual identity. You are always looking for an opportunity to investigate the unknown, to use and show your mental abilities, to find the purpose and meaning of life. You want to grow wise and to understand people and things. You need privacy to replenish your energy. You have a unique way of thinking, intuitive, reflective, and absorbing." ("What Does Name 'Pedretti' Mean,"   Seven   Reflections, http://www.sevenreflections.com/name-numerology/pedretti/)

Vener

John Venner's name was Giovanni Vener when he immigrated to Genoa. He took the American name of John, as did most Italians named Giovanni. Probably because locals pronounced his name "Ven-ner," he added an "n" to his surname. His brother Frank did not add the "n" to his

name, and his descendants still go by Vener with one "n."
In the Saint James Valley in Italy, descendants go by Vener.

Vener is an Italian name. There are some different theories
of the origin of the name, but the one I like best is: "The
surname probably derives from the translation dialect of the
personal name Venerio, attributed to the Holy Bishop
Milan in the 5th century." The venerable bishop had an
illegitimate son, and this writer subscribes to the theory that
Venners are his descendants. No proof exists that there is a
direct line, but the bishop definitely had a son who took the
surname Venerio, meaning son of the venerable bishop. (
http://www.vaol.it/it/un-cognome-alla-
settimana/vener.html)

Another theory is that the Vener ancestors' surname
used to be Baretta. In the early 1500s the son of Venero
Baretta, Giacomo, became known as Venero de Biretis. This
theory holds that James (Giacomo) became known as the
James the son of Venero instead of James of Baretta. He was
referred to as James Venerio from Paiedo, a town about
forty miles south of Campodolcino. By the time some
members of the family settled in Campodolcino sometime
in or before the 1600s, the name had evolved into Vener.
Most Veners in that region today still live in the area
around Paiedo.

Two things that are true for sure: there were Vener
families living in Portarezza, a section of Campodolcino,
during the seventeenth century, and they were Italians.
Genoa Venners can trace their roots back to one of them,
Giovanni (John) Vener, born in 1611. We even know his
father's name was Rocco Vener (aka Wener), who was born
in the 1500s.

Numerological Meaning of Vener

"You are fixed in your opinions, firm in your friendships and square in your dealings with others. You are an excellent worker. Since you are both possessive and emotional, you can be either very practical or very impractical and unpredictable. Your dual nature needs to become steadfast. You are the marrying kind. You have an eventful, exciting life. You are versatile and have the ability to learn easily.

"You are always looking for a chance to do your own thing, to be your own person, and to have things done your own way." ("What Does Name 'Vener' Mean," Seven Reflections, http://www.sevenreflections.com/name-numerology/vener/)

APPENDIX D

Pedigree as of 17 April 2009

Pedigree Chart
Michael Pedretti
Chart as of 17 April 2009

1 Michael A PEDRETTI
B: 17 Apr 1942
P: La Crosse, WI
M: 27 Oct 1990
P: Philadelphia, PA
D:
P:

Nancy HILL
(Spouse of no. 1)

2 William PEDRETTI
B: 6 Jan 1900
P: Genoa, WI
M: 15 Nov 1922
P: Genoa, WI
D: 4 Jun 1962
P: Genoa, WI

3 Agnes M. VENNER
B: 12 Apr 1903
P: Genoa, WI
D: 11 Dec 1978
P: Genoa, WI

4 Peter PEDRETTI
B: 25 Jan 1861
P: Genoa, WI
M: 26 Nov 1895
P: Genoa, WI
D: 15 Dec 1951
P: Genoa, WI

5 Margaret Marie MALIN
B: 11 Jun 1876
P: Sharpsburg, A, PA
D: 14 Sep 1921
P: La Crosse, WI

6 B "Tom" VENNER
B: 17 Nov 1873
P: Genoa, WI
M: 29 Apr 1902
P: Genoa, WI
D: 16 Apr 1946
P: Genoa, WI

7 Mary C NICOLATTI
B: 20 Feb 1880
P: Trieste, Austria
D: 18 Sep 1947
P: Genoa, WI

8 Stefano PEDRETTI
B: 15 Aug 1826
P: San Bernardo, S, Italy
M: 26 Feb 1856
P: Harmony, Bad Axe, WI
D: 1 Apr 1869
P: Genoa, WI

9 Adelaide LOMBARDI
B: 28 Jul 1830
P: Locarno, T, Switzerland
D: 10 Feb 1911
P: Genoa, WI

10 F. Joseph MALIN
B: 16 Aug 1847
P: Gofis, Austria
M: 31 Aug 1875
P: St Marys, S, A, PA
D: 7 May 1898
P: Genoa, WI

11 Margaret M GUENTNER
B: 5 Jan 1853
P: Eger, Bohemia
D: 12 Apr 1926
P: Genoa, WI

12 John Baptist G VENNER
B: 13 Mar 1829
P: Campodolcino, S, Italy
M: Abt 1867
P: Genoa, WI
D: 13 Mar 1900
P: Viroqua, Vernon, WI

13 Mary M STARLOCHI
B: 18 Apr 1849
P: Campodolcino, S, Italy
D: 10 May 1899
P: Genoa, WI

14 John M. NICHELATTI
B: 6 Apr 1850
P: Bolzano, Austria
M: 1878
P: Austria
D: 17 Aug 1932
P: La Crosse, WI

15 Margaret GABRIEL
B: 16 Feb 1855
P: Trieste, Austria
D: 23 Jul 1926
P: Genoa, WI

16 Guglielmo M PEDRETTI
B: 17 Apr 1804
M: 10 Jun 1824
D: 1 Dec 1869

17 Teresa CERLETTE
B: 27 Jan 1805
D: 9 Jan 1853

18 Peter LOMBARDI
B:
M:
D:

19 Magdalene FORMI
B:
D:

20 Josef Anton MALIN
B:
M:
D:

21 Anne Marie ERNE
B:
D:

22 Albert GUENTNER
B: 19 May 1816
M:
D: 16 Aug 1889

23 Elizabeth KRAUSE
B: 21 Jan 1832
D: 25 Sep 1914

24 Giovanni Primo VENER
B: 15 Oct 1793
M: 1 Apr 1813
D: 8 Sep 1869

25 M DELLA MORTE
B: 1793
D: 28 Jul 1842

26 B B STARLOCHI
B: 24 Sep 1825
M: 5 Mar 1847
D: 5 Aug 1900

27 Mary Ann ZABOLIO
B: 17 Dec 1823
D: 8 Feb 1905

28 Michael NICHELATTI
B:
M:
D:

29 ANTONETTE
B:
D:

30 John GABRIEL
B:
M:
D:

31 Ursula FANETTI
B:
D:

32 Guglielmo M PEDRETTI B: 7 Apr 1775
33 Marie Anna PAIAROLA B: 21 Apr 1780
34 Stefano CERLETTI B: 17 Sep 1760
35 Margherita PEDRETTI B: 25 Nov 1763
36 B:
37 B:
38 B:
39 B:
40
41 B:
42 B:
43 B:
44 B:
45 B:
46 Michael KRAUSE B:
47 B:
48 Giovanni B VENER B: 6 Mar 1749
49 Anna GHELFI B: 8 May 1750
50 G DELLA MORTE B: 10 May 1745
51 Maria P DELLA MORTE B: 12 Nov 1758
52 A G STERLOCCHI B: 18 Jul 1779
53 Maddalena GIANOLI B: 7 Oct 1781
54 F Giuseppe ZABOGLIO B: 25 May 1801
55 Maria T DP BUZZETTI B: 7 May 1797
56 B:
57 B:
58 B:
59 B:
60 B:
61 B:
62 B:
63 B:

17 April 2009

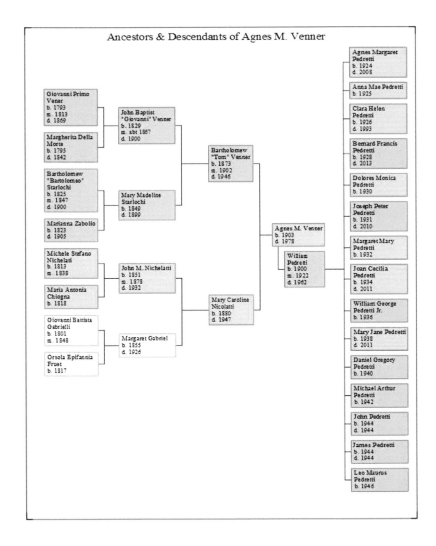

Ancestors & Descendants of Agnes M. Venner

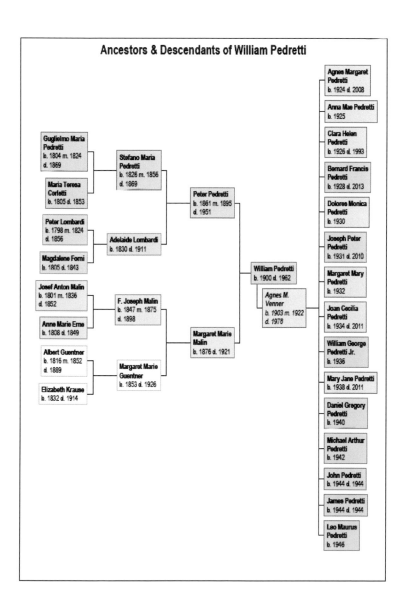

Ancestors & Descendants of William Pedretti

APPENDIX E

Charts and Maps

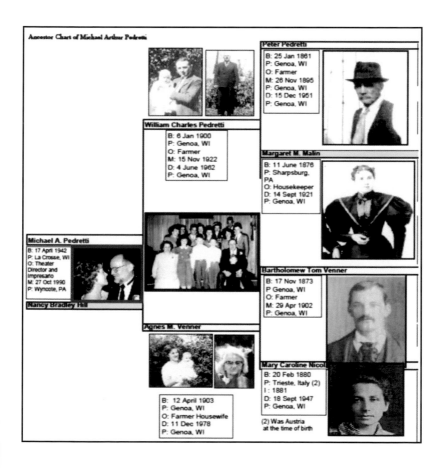

Ancestor Chart of Michael Arthur Pedretti

Peter Pedretti
B: 25 Jan 1861
P: Genoa, WI
O: Farmer
M: 26 Nov 1895
P: Genoa, WI
D: 15 Dec 1951
P: Genoa, WI

William Charles Pedretti
B: 6 Jan 1900
P: Genoa, WI
O: Farmer
M: 15 Nov 1922
D: 4 June 1962
P: Genoa, WI

Margaret M. Malin
B: 11 June 1876
P: Sharpsburg, PA
O: Housekeeper
D: 14 Sept 1921
P: Genoa, WI

Michael A. Pedretti
B: 17 April 1942
P: La Crosse, WI
O: Theater Director and Impresario
M: 27 Oct 1990
P: Wyncote, PA

Nancy Bradley Hill

Bartholomew Tom Venner
B: 17 Nov 1873
P Genoa, WI
O: Farmer
M: 29 Apr 1902
P: Genoa, WI

Agnes M. Venner
B: 12 April 1903
P: Genoa, WI
O: Farmer Housewife
D: 11 Dec 1978
P: Genoa, WI

Mary Caroline Nicol.
B: 20 Feb 1880
P: Trieste, Italy (2)
I: 1881
D: 18 Sept 1947
P: Genoa, WI

(2) Was Austria at the time of birth

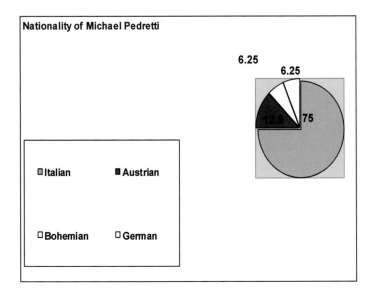

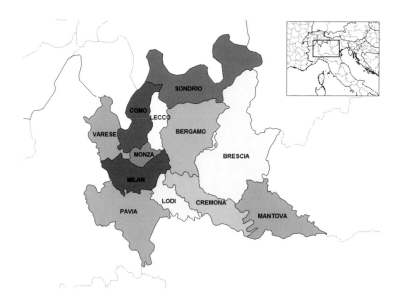

Eleven Provinces of Lombardy, including Sondrio, the center of our story

APPENDIX F

Primary Documents

Future volumes of this series will contain facsimiles of all available documents related to the characters in that volume in order to provide evidence of the family story and to provide paths for future research into our archetypic family. For this first volume in the series, I am merely introducing some examples of documents, Below is a photograph of the cover of Record of Baptisms beginning in the year 1694 maintained by the San Bernardo Church located in San Bernardo in Sondrio, Lombardy, Italy.

A photograph of the document in San Bernardo Church recording the baptism of Guglielmo Maria Pedretti on 9 April 1825. Guglielmo was the oldest of the Pedretti brothers who immigrated to Genoa, Wisconsin in 1854.

Below is a translation of the document made by the author of this book.

"In the year of our Lord one thousand eight hundred and twenty-five on the ninth day of April, I, Father Francesco Antonio Colturi, pastor of San Bernardo, baptized the infant born yesterday to Guglielmo, son of Guglielmo Pedretti and Teresa, daughter of Stefano Cerletti both of this parish. The name given is Guglielmo Maria. The godparents are Lorenzo Cerletti and Caterina Pedretti sister of the father of the infant. All are from this parish."

Baptism of Stefano Maria Pedretti (born August 15, 1826)

Above is a photograph of the record of the birth of Stefano Pedretti who immigrated to Genoa, Wisconsin with his brothers Guglielmo and Silvestro in 1854. William relocated to California prior to 1860 and Silvestro never married. All Genoa descendants of the San Bernardo Pedretti family are descendants of Stefano.

"In the year one thousand eight hundred and twenty-six on the fifteenth day of the month of August, I Father Francesco Antonio Colturi, baptize the infant born today to Guglielmo Maria Pedretti, son of another Guglielmo called "Guglielmone": and Teresa Cerletti daughter of Stefano, spouses. The name given is Stefano Maria. The godparents are Stefano Cerletti, son of another Stefano and Maria Orsola Pedretti daughter of Guglielmo."

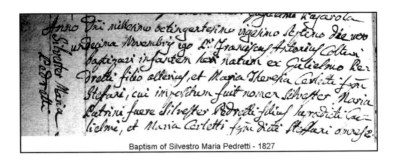

Baptism of Silvestro Maria Pedretti - 1827

In the year one thousand twenty-seven on the tenth day of November, I Father Francesco Antonio Colturi, baptize the infant born yesterday to Guglielmo Pedretti, son of Guglielmo and by Maria Teresa Cerletti, daughter of Stefano. The given name is Silvestro Maria. The godparents are Silvestro Pedretti, son of the above mentioned Guglielmo and Maria Cerletti daughter of Stefano.

APPENDIX G

Synopsis of *The Story of Our Stories*

The Story of Our Stories is the story of Maria Prima and Maria Therese, Peter and John, Adelaide and Stefano, Agnes and her children, and especially the individuals who peopled the Mount of San Bernardo and the Valley of Saint James the Lesser who turned the roughness of Bad Ax into the gentleness of Genoa, Wisconsin—but first and foremost it is our story, the story of you and me. Our story is written as an epic composed of twelve books, each with a supportive appendix. Each book covers a different measurement. Some cover the life of a typical family member of a specific generation, others reflect many people of a generation, another traces the entire story from beginning to now, and one looks into a future predicated by the behavior of our mothers. Each volume tells a critical part of the story, is an integral part of the whole, and plays into the unfolding of the epic. While arranged by number, each book can be read independent of the rest.

Book 1: *Time to Journey Home*—This is a travelogue about my trip back to the homeland and how I was inspired to write *The Story of Our Stories*. Included is part 1 of the story of rough-and-tough Bad Ax evolving into Genoa, Wisconsin—the home of a spray drift of calm and a manifesto calling for a new epic. The appendix includes a pre-1909 ahnentafel history of the author and autobiographies of select persons who researched the family's ancestry. The closing essay in this book reveals the great inequality perpetrated by the Social Security Act and offers a fail-safe solution to equalize and perpetuate Social Security ad infinitum.

Book 2: *The Veneid*—This epic poem tells of a journey into our past (similar to the *Divine Comedy*) where the poet meets many of our mothers, who celebrate woman and kindness (contrasting to the *Aeneid*'s celebration of man and war). The appendix includes the Geno outline of the female linage going back to Eve, traces the ahnentafel of the mothers, provides a chronology of major events, includes an essay on the supremacy of stories, and offers selections from *The Truly Short History of Man*.

Book 3: *Begetters of Children*—This work of historical fiction shows how the branch of one family settled on San Bernardo Mountain in Lombardy, Italy; developed a village; farmed unfarmable land; avoided plagues, wars, and other human disasters; had many children; immigrated to Genoa, Wisconsin; developed the land; and populated half of America (I joke only a little here). The appendix includes an article on the role of epic literature in shaping human perspective, a history of the founding and development of the mountain town of San Bernardo accompanied by the historical evolution of a republic government in Val San Giacomo, the ahnentafel story of Stefano Pedretti, and facsimiles of vital records of San Bernardo.

Book 4: *The Lost Book of Maria Prima della Morte*—This is an adaptation of the journal maintained by Giovanni Vener about the life and accomplishments of his grandmother Maria Prima della Morte (1758–1817). The appendix includes the ahnentafel for Giovanni Vener (born 13 March 1829), the story of Campodolcino and Val San

Giacomo, primary documents showing vital information of Giovanni's ancestors, a short work clarifying the illogicality of classism, an essay on the failure of the second amendment to protect freedom, and an article catechizing the god story.

Book 5: *L'Ultima Preghiera*—Marie Teresa Cerletti-Pedretti speaks her last prayer aloud a day or two before her death on January 29, 1853, as she realizes that her Maker has called her too early, before she can raise her family and prevent her elder sons from abandoning their heritage to the dream of a better future. The appendix tells the stories of the major churches of worship where the baptisms, marriages, and funerals of our characters took place, presents Maria Teresa's ahnentafel, explores the transitional year 1848, and includes Maria Teresa's letter to her children on the beginning of life.

Book 6: *Lettere d'Amore*—Stefano Pedretti and Adelaide Lombardi wrote a score of letters while courting each other at great distances in 1853 and 1854. The last letter is written by Adelaide forty years after she tragically lost the love of her life to a freak lumber accident. The appendix includes the ahnentafel of Adelaide Lombardi, tracing her family back to Airolo, Switzerland; the story of Airolo; primary documents of Adelaide's ancestry; photographs of our main characters' gravestones; an essay identifying the three stages of love; and observations on the immanent failure of compromise to resolve anything.

Book 7: The Diary of an Immigrant: Giovanni Vener—There are selections from the diary of a pioneer written while incarcerated in the Vernon County Insane Asylum at the turn of the century. John Venner spent the last days of his life confined, and his diary fluctuates between manic and depressed days. Readers glimpse inside of the head of an immigrant reliving the high points and the low points of being an innovator on the frontier. A highlight is the second half of the story of Genoa with a score of facsimiles of Genoa postcards. The book includes a manifesto by a great-grandchild of John calling for the end of famine, pestilence, and war—the trinity of premature death. The appendix includes the ahnentafel history of Giovanni's wife, Mary Madeline Starlochi and primary documents found during the research of the Starlochi family.

Book 8: *Peter: a Profile*—This profile describes a transitional figure who dominates his community as the world leaves the age of horse and buggy for petrol-powered mass transportation. Peter Pedretti was the wisest man I ever met. He raised eleven children, mostly by himself as his wife died shortly after the birth of their youngest daughter. The appendix includes the story of Gofis, Austria, home of the Malins and Petlarnbrand; Tochov, Bohemia, home of Maggie's mother; photos of Peter's homes and farms; the ahnentafel of Peter's wife, Maggie Malin; an essay by Peter offering a path to making an ethical life; and selections from the multi-year Sunday-morning discussions between Peter, a progressive thinker, and his conservative brother Stephen, agreeing often on goals but separated on policy and implementation.

Book 9: *The Book of Agnes*—These selections are from a novel about one of John's granddaughters, Agnes. It is a tale of the extraordinary life of one woman's gentle manner, kindness, and fertility over forty summers and forty winters, when capitalists' greed undermined the economic stability of the world, a deranged ethnic population inspired by a maniac caused the death of fifty million people, and Soviet panic all but knocked out any remaining American sense and led to numerous wrongful wars. Walt Whitman had Agnes in mind when he eulogized the "numberless unknown heroes equal to the greatest heroes known." The appendix includes mini-biographies of Agnes's siblings and in-laws; the ahnentafel chart of Agnes' mother, Mary Caroline Nicolatti; the story of Trento and Trentino, the homeland of the Nichelati family; a letter from Agnes calling us to put X back in Christmas; and a treatise asking the ultimate question: What does it mean to be human?

Book 10: *Hoe-ers: Twelve Stories by Twelve Siblings*— These autobiographies of twelve of Agnes's fifteen children are accompanied by the imagined dairies of two others. You will often read about the same events told from different perspectives. The appendix will include the story of the forty double cousins—the grandchildren Peter & Adelaide Pedretti and Tom & Mary Venner—along with the Geno story, tracing their paternal roots back to Northern Europe, the Middle East, Africa, and ultimately to Mitochondrial Adam. The concluding essay in this book will demonstrate that our worship of work—"get a job"—is nothing more than the continuation of the entitled keeping indentured serfs at service to their avarice, complemented by a tract calling for a maximum (as opposed to minimum) wage. A special section will include the creative writings of select "hoe-ers."

Book 11: *Mick: Planter of Seeds*—Selections from the author's memoirs show a farm boy becoming a college professor and going on to become an international arts festival impresario, renovator of abandon homes, and writer of this epic. The appendix will include the ahnentafel of our author covering upwards of 480 ancestors, a photo essay telling with pictures and words the story of the immigrants who played the central role of turning this story into an epic, and select primary documents from the international theater festivals made by the author. The main essay will present the revolutionary view that life on earth is made up of trinities and not of dualities or singularities.

Book 12: *Il Lavoro di Artisti*—Book 12 presents a collection of artwork created by members of the family born into the fifth generation (the grandchildren of Agnes). Their work exemplifies that this family made art instead of going to war to express their creative energy. The appendix will include the story of the children of Peter Pedretti and Bartholomew "Tom" Venner, including some fun facts about the families, a short thesis suggesting a radical reordering of representation in the US House of Representatives, and an essay demonstrating that the arts provide the exemplary methodology of education. The main piece is a manifesto by a great-grandchild of John calling for the end of nation-states, monotheism, and weapons of destruction—the primary architects of war for the past three thousand years.

Note: The contents of these books are subject to change.

End Notes

[1] There is a widely held belief that Social Security is in imminent danger and needs immediate reform, and politicians are, thankfully, afraid to touch the hot issue. I say thankfully because the proposed reforms I know about perpetuate one or more of the three big lies and will therefore only dig the system a deeper hole to fall into.

[2] Unless they and their spouse were unlucky enough to die before they reached age sixty-eight and had no qualifying children. If both worker and spouse collected, they were on the welfare payola even earlier.

[3] Daniel F. Sullivan, *A Single Index of Mortality and Morbidity, The Challenge of Epidemiology*, p. 236.

[4] This figure does not include increases in payouts.

[5] This number includes compounded interest.

[6] Don't these recipients fit the definition of the so-called "welfare mama" who collects welfare checks that are not used for food, shelter, and health, but for unessential items such as drugs, gambling, etc.? Is this any worse than retirees receiving "welfare" checks who do not need this support for food, shelter, or health but use it to help pay for a million-dollar birthday party or to hire an illegal immigrant to clean their house for an under-the-table sub-minimum wage (for which they did not pay Social Security)?

[7] Is it this legalized imbalance throughout our society more than some innate ability that condemns some to poverty while others, more favored by the law, rise to the top 1 percent?

[8] That is five times more (1.5 times more adjusted for inflation) than the value of the 1967 retiree Mr. Better-paid's "investments." Remember, he qualified for the maximum benefits. What were we thinking? True, for the value to have grown to that, Mr. Much-Less-Favored would have had to pay in the maximum for nine years. I will grant you this was unlikely, but it was possible. Does it make sense to punish someone who paid in less, considering that person's need would be all the greater?

[9] The minimum payout to those who turned sixty-seven in 2013 that "qualify" for benefits is about $431 per month; the maximum payout is $30,400 per year.

[10] I use a smaller interest rate here than when figuring 1967 as interest rates have been lower in recent years.

[11] Hopefully you noticed that Mr. Better-paid is receiving a "welfare"

check twice the minimum wage and over $2,500 more than the total salary of a worker making the median income. Ouch.

[12] If she paid in for more years, let's say forty-four years, of course it would take her longer to get her return back. But some have qualified for full benefits with less than thirty years of work. So it balances out.

[13] Annual maximum benefits are $30,396. In six years, that is a welfare payout of over $182,000 of current payroll taxes spent to support a billionaire in his retirement.

[14] "Measures of Central Tendency for Wage Data," Social Security Administration, http://www.ssa.gov/oact/cola/central.html.

[15] Isn't that the ultimate "welfare mama"?

[16] Persons making a median income of $27,915 contribute $3,461.46 in FICA tax. The employer pays half of that in theory. But there is not one employer who does not consider the total *compensation* of an employee when hiring. Employers consider the cost of "wages" plus half of FICA, health insurance, workman's compensation, and so on. In the end, all of these costs must be covered by the productivity of the worker; therefore the costs are paid for by the worker, not the employer—no more or less than the worker's "salary" is borne by the employer. So yes, each wage earner is paying for the full 12.4 percent.

[17] 2013 rate

[18] This assumes he or she works five days a week every day of the year with no unpaid holidays, vacations, or sick days.

[19] There are 14,000 households with annual incomes of over $11 million representing at least 25,000 persons who will receive the maximum Social Security benefits. While I could find no statistics, I suspect more than 3,000 are over the age sixty-six and are receiving "welfare mama" checks paid for by the poorest citizens currently in the workforce.

[20] This inequity has been the primary contributor to the growing divide between the affluent and the impoverished in America. The most affluent get a 12.3 percent flat tax reduction, and they use it to invest in property whose profits are taxed far less than earned income, thereby getting a double tax break. On the surface, that doubles the impact, but in reality it separates the poor from the "investor" exponentially. Most of us would be a lot wealthier today if we had had the same break, and the affluent would have a much smaller share of the wealth if they had paid their fair share of FICA tax. I suspect a strong case could be made that this one tax favoritism has contributed to most, if not all, of the growing inequity in income and wealth.

[21] Of course, the Social Security office is not demanding its investments be returned but instead is using the dollars they collect this month to pay the recipients getting money within the next thirty days. The Social

Security surplus has long been spent by the federal government for general operating expenses. Will they be able to pay their debt when the day comes that Social Security takes in less than it spends and demands payment?

[22] In 2013 the maximum FICA, including the employer "half," was $14,098, and benefits for someone who retired at full retirement age is $2,533, or $30,396 per year. More than ten million American households have incomes below $12,000.

[23] To help motivate all who can comfortably live without benefits, we should offer them choices for how their benefits can be used. On a simple check-off form, they could indicate if they want their benefits to revert back to the general Social Security fund, support the SAVE program (described later), or be added to a special account set to provide additional retirement funds for children born into families who are living in poverty. Since Americans fear capping the unearned Social Security benefits of the wealthiest citizens, let's at least make it easy for the wealthy to better put those funds to use.

We should also offer the opportunity for the retired affluent to replace past welfare benefits they collected. These were not payments they earned or deserved. The correct thing is for them to be returned with interest to the Social Security fund. Likewise, those with total gross adjusted incomes over the maximum FICA charge should have the opportunity to pay up for the past free ride they had. While it may be unrealistic to expect a full refund of 12.4 percent, the full rate up to 6.2 percent that was due when earnings were acquired is past due.

[24] The current poverty line is $11,490, and 150 percent of that is $17,235. A good working number for inflation based on history over sixty-six years is 7.6 times. With that data we arrive at a need of $17,235, multiplied by 7.6, which equals a little over $130,000 per year that 2079 retirees will need.

[25] Returns for S&P 500 have been consistently over 10 percent per annum for any sixty-six-year period. By being forced to balance the ratio of securities and bonds, the trustees should be able to do better than the S&P average. I pick 8 percent per annum to be conservative and to have a stronger likelihood of beating projections.

[26] $15,000 times 4 million newly born equals $60 billion.

[27] The American public has a contract with the government called the Constitution. In return for the government's efforts to "form a more perfect union, establish justice, insure domestic tranquility, provide for the common defense, promote the general welfare, and secure the blessings of liberty to ourselves and our posterity," the US citizen pays a tax. When the rich opt out of this contract and, instead of paying tax, lend the money (by investing in bonds and treasuries) to the

government so they can receive public services, they not only break their end of the contract but extort the government by demanding that future generations pay their offspring back the "loan" with interest that should have been collected as taxes. This further separates those who overpay for services and those who "lend" money to the government for the services they receive. That is a nice racket: instead of paying for services, the wealthiest lend money to the government to cover the costs of services and, after services are rendered, demand the money back with interest. I'd like to be able to receive services and make purchases with that financial arrangement. Let's say I want to buy a $650 computer from Dell Computer. I pay up front 65 cents (one-tenth of one percent of the cost) and lend Dell $649.35 to cover the rest of the cost. I then use the computer for three years and toss it in the junk. I remind Dell they borrowed $649.35 and that they must pay their debt to me with interest. I like that arrangement. You can see why the richest Americans like their current arrangement with the government, create myths claiming they pay in more, and spend a few million to elect politicians who will perpetuate the arrangement where they can buy bonds with the money they "saved" through unconscionable tax breaks. This abdication of responsibility could easily account for the entire federal debt. That is not to say there are no other contributing factors. In truth, the government could offer more services, most people could pay less in taxes, and there could be an operating surplus if this and other inequities were eliminated.

[28] Based on 3 percent average inflation, they will need benefit checks of $51,000 or a supplement of $13,000 to their projected Social Security package when the current batch retires in 2038. They will need about $200,000 in their SAVE at retirement time. There are approximately 4.1 million citizens age thirty-three, meaning this late action to correct only 25 percent of the shortfall will cost almost what the full correction costs at birth—only meaning it all the more urgent we act now. The total cost for this phase, which will continue for the entire thirty-three years to correct the current scheme, will be about 52 billion dollars per year in today's money. In other words, the total cost of both SAVE accounts could be covered by the 1 percent of households making the largest incomes paying 4.6 percent in FICA tax; that is just 37 percent of what you and I pay in FICA tax.

[29] I'd prefer America to completely replace the current system in twenty-two years, by creating accounts for the next twenty-two years for every American on their twenty-second and forty-fourth birthday. By the time this year's babies turn twenty-two, everyone will be covered, and the program can be maintained indefinitely for a mere $60 billion (in today's money) for those born in any given year. This could

be accomplished by every American paying 12.4 percent of their income as FICA tax. Given the poorest have been doing that since 1990, it seems the wealthiest could handle paying their fair share going into the future. On the other hand, we could keep lower rates for all if the wealthiest Americans were willing to create fully funded accounts for every American as they turn twenty-two and forty-four. In order to do this, the affluent would have to recognize that a large portion of their accumulated wealth is the result of underpaying their fair share of FICA for the past seventy-six years. By making partial retroactive payment into the fund from their accumulated wealth, they could underwrite this cost for the next twenty-one years. This would involve a complex formula to exchange stock, etc., from their portfolios to individual citizens. Forty-four-year-olds would need $350,000 accounts, and twenty-two-year-olds $75,000 accounts. This would cost $1.7 trillion dollars per year—well within the means of the wealthiest Americans. I know this is unlikely to happen, but if the wealthy decided to accept the responsibility to meet their part of the contract with the country, the plan to return a portion of their ill-gotten wealth to the public would have to be carefully implemented to avoid unforeseen consequences that might affect the stability of our economic system.

[30] When I survey students asking on the first day of class if they think they should pay higher taxes for work, inheritance, or investment, nearly 100 percent, including the most conservative, say labor should be taxed at the lowest rate and inheritance at the highest rate. This is not a scientific study, but I have no doubt a well-conducted national survey would produce similar results. Why, then, has America propagated an inverse system where wages are taxed by far the most, defying the will and the logic of the public as revealed by these students?

[31] Note: if the surplus for the fund gets too large, rates for the lower quintiles can be lowered; or better, the special fund for those born into poverty can be enlarged, or current retirees who are in most need can be given higher benefits.

[32] If the wealthy mount propaganda campaign and convince the American public this is not equitable, they should stand ashamed. However, if they do that, the total cost of the SAVE initiative could be covered by the top 1 percent of the top 1 percent (that is, the 14,000 most highly paid households in America) paying 13.8 percent of their income in FICA tax. That is less than 1.5 percent more than you pay. The top 10 percent of the top 1 percent of taxpayers (135,000 households with an average income of $3.9 million) could pay for this program by only paying 11.4 percent FICA tax, or 1 percent less than you pay. If the top 1 percent of the top 1 percent paid for 50 percent of the cost, they would pay only 6.9 percent, and if the next 9 percent of

the top 1 percent of earners paid the other 50 percent, they would be paying only 6.3 percent to FICA (versus your 12.4 percent). Isn't that the least they could do for the future of the country that made it possible for them to be so successful, and a small repayment for having been given a scot-free ride for the first seventy-six years of Social Security? I am not proposing that those earning more than 99.9 percent of Americans should carry the entire burden. As shown elsewhere, both SAVE funds could be funded, the current system strengthened, and rates reduced for all Americans by instituting a more equitable tax base.

[33] Owners were able to decide if they wanted to invest 25, 50, or 75 percent of their fund in securities. The balance was invested in bonds or cash. The new, improved TIAA-CREF system seems to have had poorer returns for most investors. The default plan should be to put 75 percent in stocks at birth, change to 50 percent at age fifty, and 25 percent at age sixty. The entire fund should be converted to government-held bonds at retirement. It should also be noted that one of the reasons for providing retirement benefits is to have recipients retire, thereby opening up work opportunities for the next generation. It is not a wise use of human resources to keep young people out of the workforce, thereby failing to offer them the opportunity to become more effective workers as they gain experience.

[34] Since the SAVE account was set up to cover retirement and not offspring after one's death, no one can claim they deserve its value at death; since the owner did not personally contribute to the fund, he or she has no claim on its value at death; since society provided funds for the account, it deserves to get back the full value at the owner's death.

[35] Add this proposal to Matthew Miller's *The 2 Percent Solution* and we may be on our way to recovery from arguably the biggest era of greed known to humankind. Neither of us is asking any significant sacrifices, but relying instead on the common-sense response of all Americans to ideas that offer solutions equal to the problems with full awareness of the power of the current political and greed systems.

[36] Williams wrote "grief" where I transposed "greed" as he was talking about death and a funeral. We are talking about life and equality and what keeps them from bringing happiness to more people.